MEANING WELL IS NOT ENOUGH

Perspectives on Volunteering

JANE MALLORY PARK

ISBN NUMBERS: Hard cover 0-916068-17-X
Soft cover 0-916068-18-8

Published by  GROUPWORK
TODAY, INC.

Post Office Box 258
South Plainfield, N. J. 07080

Printed and bound in the U.S.A.

DEDICATED TO MY PARENTS WHOSE EXAMPLE LED
ME INTO THIS VOLUNTEERING BUSINESS AND WITH
SPECIAL APPRECIATION TO MY HUSBAND AND SONS
WHO HAVE LIVED WITH ME THROUGH THE UPS
AND DOWNS OF MANY VOLUNTEER ADVENTURES
AND LOVED ME ANYWAY.

CONTENTS

SECTION III: EFFECTIVE VOLUNTEERING: PERSPECTIVES FOR THE FUTURE

1

A PERSONAL PERSPECTIVE -- AND WHERE IT LED

1.1 OCCUPATION: DO-GOODER

"Do-gooder" is not an official occupational title on anybody's list. Yet in many ways it is a fair description of the activities which have made up a significant portion of my adult life. It might be nice to be able to say that I intentionally set out to become a do-gooder in order to save the world or at least make it a little better. Certainly the aura of saintliness, self-sacrifice, and martyrdom which such intentionality implies is not entirely unattractive. But the truth of the matter is that I made a series of self-serving life choices which might just as easily have led to a career in loansharking, had I been in a different place at a different time.

To begin with, I was raised by two parents who believed that community service was a natural part of one's adult obligations and acted on that belief. My physician father concentrated his volunteer efforts in community health concerns. My mother participated in a wide range of volunteer activities, always including but never restricted to those involving her children. When her twenty-five years of dedicated involvement in the PTA led to her selection as its national president, I naturally felt a daughter's pride. I also had an opportunity to see first-hand some very sophisticated, high-powered volunteer work. It was out of step with the "just a volunteer" pat on the head which I had thought applied only to youth volunteers but which I was beginning to see was used on adults too. The PTA presidency had moments of glamour such as having coffee with the President of the United States to discuss educational issues, and it entailed much grueling work such as presiding over a ten-hour floor debate on busing among a thousand delegates. In her "retirement" this energetic woman resumed community-based volunteer work including four years as a den mother for her grandsons.

Meanwhile I pursued an undergraduate degree in sociology and went on to complete a Master of Social Work degree in community organization. For a few years after that I served as adult program director for a community YWCA and was, for a short time, a staff associate at the local social planning agency. When family considerations precipitated my "retirement" from paid professional do-gooding, it seemed only natural to use my social service interests, training and skills in a variety of volunteer capacities made available by many different kinds of organizations.

Many of my volunteer assignments have been quite routine: PTA room mother and officer, assistant Cub Scout den mother, children's choir director, Sunday School teacher, volunteer recruiter and co-ordinator for Girl Scouts and church. Since the groups I have been involved with are always at or near a subsistence level of funding, I have found it necessary and, to my surprise, exhilarating to join in money-raising activities ranging from bake sales and bazaars to solicitation for annual operating funds to chairing divisions in operating and capital fund-raising campaigns.

With an enthusiasm which many people find perverse, I have thrived as a member of numerous committees and boards of one kind or another. I am especially attracted to study, long-range planning and organizational self-evaluation activities, the more complicated and controversial the better. A three-year stint as president of the local YWCA during which the organization completed a million dollar capital campaign, renovated its building, and changed executive directors, in addition to maintaining its usual operation, was filled with some of the greatest rewards and frustrations I had ever encountered. It marked a culmination of sorts in what might be called a volunteer career.

There is no denying that at various points this volunteer workload and commitment equalled or surpassed the time and energy one might expect to devote to a job. However, I was often just too busy to worry about what being a volunteer meant. In the back of my mind I knew that in its best moments the volunteer work I did was more personally gratifying than the paid positions I had held or was likely to find in the geographic area to which I am confined by virtue of my husband's employment. At its most frustrating, I did wonder why I bothered, and in one or two instances I did quit. Isn't that just like a volunteer?

Yet one cannot knock around the volunteering business without picking up vibrations about the issues surrounding the proper role of volunteers. I read much of the literature at one time or another but usually for an immediate purpose in a given organization. Over the years I became aware that not all was well in the do-gooding sector and that the status of volunteering was one of the problems. I also learned that the volunteer work I was doing and seeing was painfully typical of that going on all over.

The one thought which remained clear throughout these experiences was that I resented the label of "do-gooder" which applied in my case to both my paid and volunteer activities. Part of the discomfort stemmed from being aware that doing good implies a selflessness which, as already stated, was not necessarily so. It also implies that one is interfering in affairs or in the lives of others where one does not belong. While I understood the source of this feeling, it never quite made sense that doing good sounded worse than doing bad. Above all, do-gooding is a phrase which people employ when they feel they have to say something nice and cannot think of anything substantive to praise. Particularly when addressing a volunteer, people are often either reluctant to criticize at all or at least want to soften their criticisms. The handy way to do that is to preface remarks with "Well, they meant well." In response to that approach, I have often wanted to scream, "Meaning well is not enough. Let us talk about whether or not all this do-gooding is doing any good. Let us talk results, not intentions." For the most part, however, I and many of my paid and volunteer colleagues who share this concern have suppressed the scream and postponed dealing with that issue to a less demanding time.

Naturally such a time never comes by itself; it has to be created. When a hiatus occurred after completing a major volunteer commitment, I put myself on "sabbatical" and decided to pursue in a serious and systematic way the general subject of volunteering and its status. This launched a sojourn which would lead from introspection to reflection to analysis of the subject as it had been addressed by the "experts" and finally to some insights about where we might go from here and how. As you have guessed by now, this sojourn in good sabbatical fashion is recorded here.

1.2 EVERYBODY KNOWS WHAT VOLUNTEERING IS

Or do they? If there ever was a subject which people take for granted and on which they consider themselves experts, it is volunteerism. Yet I was to find that one of the first hurdles in studying the subject was to define the term volunteer. I was not satisfied with the quick "unpaid do-gooding" response which I got from many people I asked. After weeks of thought and research, I concluded that the precision I

was seeking was not that of a doctoral dissertation but
one which encompassed variables encountered in practice
and which allowed for exploration of different
issues. With that in mind, I propose the following
definition for the purposes of our discussion:

> A volunteer is an individual who chooses to
> participate in activities perceived by that
> person to promote human welfare, human dig-
> nity, and social justice when those activi-
> ties--are not the source of one's liveli-
> hood,--require involvement beyond what is
> expected of all citizens (e.g., voting) or of
> all members of an organization (e.g., paying
> dues), and--are conducted in a manner con-
> sistent with the ideals of a free, democratic,
> pluralistic society.

If you think this was easy, you can try defining
the word in a useful way with twenty-five words or less,
and/or you can explore the more academic approach to
defining it which is presented in Appendix A. Both
exercises are recommended. In the meantime, let me be
the first to acknowledge that this definition is broad
and by design leaves considerable latitude for the
wide-ranging, free-wheeling discussion of volunteering
which follows.

Another thing everybody knows is what volunteers
do: "unpaid do-gooding." Here again it is useful to be
a bit more precise than that, and I will be using the
following terms:

Direct Service--work in which the volunteer provides
services to the client group of an
organization or to the persons perceived
to be in need. e.g., counseling, being
an ombudsman, advising groups and neighboring.

Organization Maintenance--work performed for an organization perceived by the volunteer to be
promoting human welfare, etc., but which
does not involve the volunteer directly
with the client group of that organization. e.g., public relations, fundraising, clerical work.

Policy Development--work conducted by groups (boards, committees, task forces) within an organization leading to the establishment of policies and procedures which enable the organization to fulfill its mission.

Social Action/Advocacy--activities aimed at promoting a social cause and/or generating organizational and institutional changes perceived by the volunteer to be beneficial to a class of individuals with a common need/concern. These activities can be conducted on one's own or in an organization.

1.3 AT LEAST WE KNOW WHAT BEING A VOLUNTEER MEANS

Actually everybody who has been or has known a volunteer is an expert on this one. The problems and possibilities inherent in volunteerism manifest themselves in everyday occurrences in many blatant and subtle ways. The examples below are typical of the flashes of insight we have all experienced when we know exactly what being a volunteer means. They come under the heading of "You know what being a volunteer means when . . ."

. . .you are called by a school nurse and asked to deliver an emergency food basket. You drag your children along because there is no one to babysit. You find a clean but barren apartment and a mother who is a deaf mute. As you leave, the mother smiles and makes a sound which the daughter translates as "thank you." Your children ask why the lady talked funny, but the lump in your throat prohibits a response.

. . .you find out that your food basket bought some time for the school nurse to contact the welfare department for long-term help. You are glad you were there to fill in that crack, but you wonder why it was there to begin with and who is working on that.

. . .you deliver another food basket to another family and discover they are amassing food from a variety of

6

charitable sources in order to have a party, and you feel abused.

. . .your work day or your supper hour is interrupted by a lengthy phone call about a volunteer project, and you wish you had an office for your volunteer work and office hours to protect you.

. . .you fill out your income tax form and realize that the mileage deduction for volunteering is substantially less than that for business, and you had always assumed that the car depreciated, needed oil and maintenance, and had to be insured regardless of the reasons it was being driven.

. . .on the same form, you add up all your volunteer expenses, realize that the money would have paid for a nice holiday, but are glad at least that you benefit from itemizing deductions.

. . .you are told by the person whom everyone thinks is the best candidate to succeed you in a job that she cannot afford to absorb those expenses, deductible or not, and the agency cannot afford to reimburse her--or thinks it cannot.

. . .you find that many of the feminist arguments against women doing volunteer work make infinite sense, but among the volunteer jobs you have enjoyed most is being in charge of the "ladies" who cook church dinners, thus having a socially acceptable outlet for your "bossy" instincts.

. . .you are completing your Census form, are asked if you worked last week, and are told to answer "no" if what you did was volunteer work or housework.

. . .you notice that men are often put in volunteer leadership positions by virtue of their business relationships and women have to "earn" leadership via the tea and cookie route.

. . .you realize that volunteer training is taken most seriously in groups where women predominate but you have not noticed that this can be justified on grounds that men automatically perform as effective volunteers and therefore do not need it.

. . .you listen to the speaker at the Volunteer Recognition Dinner praise volunteers to the sky, and you find it hard to believe this is the same person who always forgets you are coming, never knows what to do with you when you arrive, and then is heard to complain that one cannot count on volunteers.

. . .you resent the notion that volunteers are unreliable but have gotten yourself into one volunteer job that is so distasteful you find yourself praying for a foot of snow, a sick child or some other plausible excuse not to go in.

. . .as either staff or volunteer, you are recruiting volunteer help and are turned down by people who simply do not have the time. Yet you know they manage to play golf three times a week, and you begin to think they have the right idea.

. . .you are frantically recruiting and you issue a plea for help at a meeting whereupon the least desirable candidate for the task volunteers. Now you are stuck; volunteers cannot be turned down or fired.

. . .a piece of legislation you and your cohorts have lobbied hard for is finally passed and your legislator attributes it to the barrage of mail you engineered.

. . .while serving on the boards of three nonprofit organizations, you read that a former President is serving on three for-profit boards and being paid $60,000 for shouldering the same legal and ethical responsibilities that you have.

This list, while lengthy, is not complete. It is sufficient, however, to provide grounds for reasserting my contention that these moments of truth speak clearly about the meaning of volunteering in society today. What they say clearly is that there is a great deal of ambivalence about and among volunteers. We have not really decided if volunteers are priceless or worthless. As a result there are inconsistencies between what we say about the joys and importance of volunteering and what we do with it in specific situations. Some of this stems from fuzzy attitudes; some from sloppy, almost to the point of casual, policies and practices. Yet the same discrepancies arise even in groups which are putting considerable effort into making efficient and effective use of volunteers. This suggests that the roots of the problem may go deeper than those of any one volunteer program in any one organization. For help on this we must turn not only to our own experiences but also to other expert sources.

1.4 RESOURCES TO USE AND ABUSE

A considerable body of literature is building on the subject of volunteering. Most of it is interesting to contemplate, and much of it is also useful if hauled off the shelf in the right place at the right time. The literature tends to fall into three categories, each of which serves a different purpose.

1.4a Trend-oriented Advocates

Many students of volunteering focus on measuring and documenting the scope of volunteerism. Some take an historical approach, carefully reviewing the annals for evidence that volunteering has played a significant role in the nation's development. As it turns out, the evidence is there and does confirm our generally held belief that volunteerism has been a pervasive phenomenon and that its value is not a figment of our imaginations or a cultural myth. An excellent example of this approach is the work of Susan J. Ellis and Katherine H. Noyes as presented in "By The People: A History of Americans as Volunteers."[1] Unlike the average history text where the evidence is present but buried, Ellis and Noyes emphasize that volunteering has been a quiet, sustained, cumulative response by large numbers of unknown citizens as well as the more dramatic involvement in crusades where the leaders' names are well-known.

Other analysts take a statistical approach using modern data gathering and assessment techniques. Until recently the most complete and still the most often cited effort of this nature was a 1974 survey commissioned by ACTION, the federal agency responsible

for such volunteer programs as VISTA and the Peace
Corps, and conducted by the United States Census
Bureau. This study revealed that 37 million or one out
of four Americans over the age of thirteen did some form
of volunteer work. Compared with a similar study
conducted in 1965, this represented a 6% increase in the
portion of the total population participating in
volunteer work. Volunteer work was defined in this
study as unpaid work for organizations in such fields as
religion, health, education, civic and community action,
recreation, social welfare, politics, and justice. These volunteers, representing a cross-section of
the total population in terms of age and socio-economic
background, averaged nine hours per week of service. This was the equivalent of adding 3.5 million
full-time workers to the labor market, then numbering 85
million.[2] The value of the work contributed was later
estimated to have been around $34 billion.[3]

In 1981, INDEPENDENT SECTOR, a national forum to
encourage giving, volunteering and not-for-profit
initiative, asked the Gallup Organization to take a
survey of volunteering. For this survey, INDEPENDENT
SECTOR broadened the definition of volunteering to
include helping activities done alone or informally as
well as the more traditional formal activities. The
survey showed that by this more inclusive definition,
53% of American adults and 53% of teenagers did at least
some volunteer work in the year between March, 1980 and
March, 1981. By separating out formal (organized)
volunteering from informal services, the survey reports
that 31% of the population averaged two or more
volunteer hours per week in organized settings, and 10%
averaged seven or more hours weekly. Like the previous
surveys, this one found that a wide socio-economic range
of the population does volunteer work in an endless
variety of settings and tasks.[4] INDEPENDENT SECTOR
later calculated the value of volunteer services
performed at $64.5 billion.[5]

Also individual national organizations keep records
and issue reports about the number of volunteers
participating in their programs. From the IRS data on
the proliferation of nonprofit groups where volunteer
participation is assumed and from other reporting
sources, it is quite reasonable and accurate to conclude

10

that volunteering remains a significant reality in today's world. Coming at the subject from a different angle, a Gallup Poll conducted in the late 1970's among urban residents revealed that 80% of those surveyed would be willing to get involved in their communities if asked.[6] The possibility that this gap between the numbers of people who would volunteer and those who really do is true of the entire population can certainly warm the hearts of volunteer recruiters.

I have not done justice here to all the data which is available. Its collection and analysis are fraught with many interesting obstacles to accuracy and with severe limitations when used for comparative purposes. These are described for interested parties in Appendix B. You may be more troubled by having the trend-oriented folks labeled as advocates. This implies that the research has not been conducted in an appropriately objective manner, and that is an unfair inference. Certainly the statistician-types have identified the definitions used, the parameters of measurement techniques, and any resulting limitations on the data gathered. The reason for the "advocate" label is that most of the studies have been conducted by and for groups which are very interested in promoting volunteerism and which use the data to assure us that we are not trying to keep a sinking ship afloat. This is not all bad, except that measures of quantity seem to lead to a "more-is-by-definition-better" perception. One has to wonder if the data would be so gleefully reported if 90% of Americans volunteered but directed their voluntary energies at terrorist causes, although, if true, we would certainly need to know it. In other words, preoccupation with quantity can lead to assumptions about quality which do not hold true. Statistical and other trend-oriented information is important and useful as long as we remember that assurances, however well documented, that volunteerism is very much alive do not automatically mean that it is well.

1.4b "How-To" Advocates

Perhaps the most popular pieces of volunteer literature are the numerous manuals, guidelines, and other tools which almost invariably have a "how-to" somewhere in their titles. Often these resources are directed at specific types of volunteering in specific settings and outline the steps which, if followed diligently, will lead to more effective use of volunteers in those settings.

The "how-to" advocates start with the assumption that volunteering is good and healthy both for the individual volunteer and society as a whole. They acknowledge that problems exist but believe that the roots are not in the basic concept but rather in its implementation. Difficulties are perceived as resulting from the misuse of volunteers, misunderstandings about motivation, inadequate recruitment and training, and, last but most definitely not least, the undervaluing and underappreciating of voluntary efforts. Volunteers, after all, mean well. If "they" are at times bumbling and ineffective, it is because "we" have not managed them properly and/or stroked them often enough. If not enough people are volunteering, that is because "we" have not been sufficiently creative in competing with the other options "they" have for the use of their free time.

Here again, the problem is not so much that the ideas presented are not valid and useful. As far as they go, they are very constructive and rational approaches to some real problems organizations face in maintaining and improving their operations. Sometimes, however, their approach is so simplistic it makes the volunteers sound like plastic wind-up toys. This can be more than a little patronizing and counterproductive. More importantly, they often do not go far enough in helping an organization assess its readiness and receptivity to the changes proposed. If the organization has a firm handle on its overall purpose, has a clearly stated mission, and is generally well-managed, a "how-to" approach to the use of volunteers can be a real shot in the arm. If it is not, the "how-to" is merely a placebo easing only one symptom of a more systemic disease. It is rarely a magical cure for the symptom or the disease.

Finally, the ten-easy-steps mentality diverts an organization from doing difficult soul-searching and hard thinking not only about ways of enhancing its own

12

survival but also about whether that survival is justified and urgent when measured against the larger context of community needs. Few people want to open that can of worms. It is easier to keep busy and look efficient by abusing the "how-to" literature.

1.4c The Critics

Not all analysts of the volunteer scene have reached happy and optimistic conclusions about the subject.[7] Critics have claimed that, good intentions notwithstanding, volunteers have engaged in needless and even harmful meddling in the lives of others. Do-gooders have often been patronizing to a fault in their efforts to aid the less fortunate by imposing their own values and methods on the individuals they seek to serve. Volunteers, particularly those attempting to alleviate human suffering directly, have been accused also of perpetuating an inequitable status quo. They are, it is argued, using first aid on social ills which require at the very least major surgery on existing institutions or, better yet, the "preventive" medicine of new social orders. By their very willingness to take these misguided steps without pay, volunteers are demeaning themselves as well as the objects of their charity and are thereby compounding the very problems they hope to resolve.

Social action volunteers, many of whom have accepted this school of criticism as valid particularly for direct service volunteering, have had their personal motivations questioned on psychological as well as political grounds. It has been a shock for some volunteers to be accused of empire building, power grabbing and glory seeking when the stated object of their efforts has not been self-aggrandizement but stamping out evil or correcting injustice. Nonetheless, such assessments have been made and deserve consideration.

Focusing on the damage done by volunteers to themselves and society, critics have been less likely than advocates to offer elaborate "how-to" suggestions. They often, however, either explicitly or implicitly propose a simple solution to the issues raised: "Scrap volunteering. If volunteers are doing such important and necessary work, society will find a way to get it done properly." They have not, in many instances, been particularly precise about why volunteering is not a proper activity in our society or how, if we should not continue to live with volunteering, we are going to live without it or get from here to there. For example, if in fact volunteers of their own free will performed $64.5 billion of services in a recent year, how much of this would the critics have been glad to pay in additional taxes or charitable contributions?

Volunteer advocates often respond to the critics with an indignant, knee-jerk rebuttal or a quavering "yes, but . . .." Either response abuses this brand of literature by encouraging us to gloss over the many valid issues being raised. Actually the so-called anti-volunteer literature is in many ways the most insightful and helpful to those who feel that volunteerism should be kept and cultivated as a positive force in society.

To sum up, our experiences raise many questions and concerns which deserve consideration. The literature available points in promising directions but raises as many questions as it answers. It appears that there is more to be said and heard, more to be learned and tested in practice.

1.5 A CAVEAT AND AN INVITATION

Despite the first-person, chatty nature of this introductory chapter, I hope it is clear by now that this work is not intended to be the autobiography of a vacuous volunteer. Nor, alas, will it be THE definitive diagnosis and cure for what is ailing volunteerism today. It is designed to reexamine the subject and present it in a different context for the purpose of evoking insights, provoking discussions, and pointing up some new avenues for action. It is an attempt to put what we already know about "how-to" into a context of "how come" and "why bother."

If the cursory review of the literature and all this talk about Appendices seemed a little heavy and/or removed from reality, I must warn you that things will get worse before they get better. We are, after all, attempting to get a handle on a subject which affects the values, social relationships, and institutional structures of society as we know it or would like it to become. Because it is all too easy to see the trees for the forest, I must also caution you that it is necessary to pull back from immediate concerns to try to gain new perspective. To that end, I will remove the first person and, when absolutely necessary to interject myself again, do so as "the writer."

You are invited to participate in this exercise if you care enough about what happens to volunteering to look at the subject in its complexity. If you are willing to set aside for the moment your immediate problems and take a broader and deeper look at today's situation and how it developed, and if, having done that, you are willing to weigh your own attitudes and practices against that larger context for clues about what happens from here, you are ready to accept the invitation. At rock bottom, this effort is for those of us who know that meaning well is not enough.

REFERENCES

[1] Susan J. Ellis and Katherine H. Noyes, BY THE PEOPLE: A HISTORY OF AMERICANS AS VOLUNTEERS (Philadelphia: ENERGIZE, 1978).

[2] U.S., Bureau of the Census, AMERICANS VOLUNTEER 1974: A STATISTICAL STUDY OF VOLUNTEERS IN THE UNITED STATES (Washington, D.C.: ACTION, February, 1975), pp. 3-4.

[3] Harold Wolozin, THE VALUE OF VOLUNTEER SERVICES IN THE UNITED STATES (Washington, D.C.: ACTION, September, 1976), ACTION Pamphlet No. 35304, pp. 15-16.

[4] The Gallup Organization, Inc., AMERICANS VOLUNTEER 1981: A STUDY CONDUCTED FOR INDEPENDENT SECTOR (Princeton, N.J.: The Gallup Organization, June, 1981), pp. iv-v.

[5]INDEPENDENT SECTOR, News Release, Washington, D.C., January 7, 1982, p. 2.

[6]As cited by Kerry Kenn Allen, "Volunteering in America, 1980-81," VOLUNTARY ACTION LEADERSHIP, Winter, 1981, p. 6.

[7]Doris B. Gold, OPPOSITION TO VOLUNTEERISM: AN ANNOTATED BIBLIOGRAPHY, CPL Bibliography No. 8 (Chicago: Council of Planning Librarians, June, 1979).

SECTION I

PERSPECTIVES FROM THE PAST

2

SOCIETY'S STEP-CHILDREN

2.1 THE CITIZEN VOLUNTEER

The definition of volunteer we are using indicates
that citizens become volunteers when they move into
areas of social concern beyond what is normally expected
or required. They differ from nonvolunteer citizens in
at least two significant ways. The first is the
volunteer's stated or assumed belief that individuals
have a responsibility to participate actively as members
of society and to help make that society more responsive
to the needs of its members. Secondly, volunteers
believe that individual action will make a difference
and that the social condition being addressed will
respond to conscious intervention by concerned

persons. In other words, the volunteer type does not believe that whatever exists is what must be and does believe that action beyond the wringing of hands and gnashing of teeth is both imperative and appropriate. We are not debating here whether they have been correct in these assumptions but merely stating that this kind of conviction is an important distinction between the volunteer and the nonvolunteer.

Our definition also deals with activity perceived to promote human welfare, human dignity, and social justice. Opinions as to what constitutes an acceptable level of welfare, dignity, or justice have changed throughout history. However, certain themes do recur which are relevant to understanding what volunteers have done and why they have done it.

First, we must keep in mind that this country was settled and the nation founded on the belief that individuals are entitled to life, liberty and the pursuit of happiness. What was perceived as needed was a social structure which permitted individuals to achieve those goals and not a nation of individuals whose reason for existence was to perpetuate the social structure. Every new trend, particularly where government involvement was at issue, was eyed with suspicion for its potential threat to people's capacity to shape their own destinies. If it passed that test, it was pursued enthusiastically and often unquestioningly.

While this ideal of individualism seems clear enough, it has proved to be complicated because our legal and social definitions of which persons are entitled to these pursuits have changed. For example, blacks and women were excluded for a time. Furthermore, our understanding of the intended and unintended impact of various social institutions on individual liberty has changed. We now realize that forces other than government can influence individual freedom for better or worse.

A second theme is more of a recurring tension, for the ideal of individual freedom and self-sufficiency has been tempered by awareness that independence and dependence are relative terms. We are all to some degree dependent on others at different points in our

19

lives and for different reasons. Some factors which reduce or preclude individual self-reliance can be viewed as not being the individual's own "fault:" childhood, old age, and most physical illnesses. Others raise the question of whether or not society iself creates the dependency problem it abhors: crime, poverty, mental illness. Obviously, definitions of which kinds of dependency fall in each category have varied among political and religious outlooks as well as with the state of scientific knowledge. From these variations in definition have sprung equally diverse responses to perceived problems. Though the debate still rages over the extent of society's responsibility to alleviate or correct dependency problems, there has been general agreement that independence is the norm and dependence the object of concern or suspicion.

Quality of life is another theme with several levels of meaning but relevant, nonetheless, to the motivation of volunteers. One era's luxury is another era's necessity, e.g., public education. What to one person is an essential ingredient for the good life is considered a dispensable frill by others, e.g., arts and recreation. Some sets of volunteers have been busy promoting human dignity by enriching community life beyond basic survival and other groups equally busy resisting efforts to make the community responsible for these extra touches.

The brief sweep through American social history which follows is intended to point up examples of the kinds of societal tensions which volunteer activity has both reflected and shaped. It is only moderately chronological and is mainly intended to be a thematic review of those pieces of history which contribute most to an understanding of volunteering today.

It is this writer's contention that the degree of acceptance, ambivalence or hostility of the general public toward the issues being addressed has had much to do with society's attitudes about the volunteers who are involved with those issues. Where the volunteer's active involvement reflects a generally held conviction that a perceived situation is a problem, the difference between volunteers and nonvolunteers is only that one group chooses to act. These volunteers earn reputations as good citizens, civic leaders, or heroes.

In other cases, the volunteers' perception of need puts them out of step with prevailing social opinion and places them in the vanguard of those identifying problems, working on solutions, and attempting thereby to enlist public recognition of the legitimacy of both needs and proposed corrective actions. Volunteers and the causes they espouse often become society's stepchildren. They are acknowledged as part of the family but remain vulnerable to hostility, acceptance, or points in between. Some terms which have been used to describe these volunteers cannot be tastefully recorded here. Others such as "do-gooder" or "amateur" lose their punch when printed, because tone of voice reveals more than the words themselves. In all cases, historical variations on the theme "volunteer" offer important insights into the status of volunteerism today.

2.2 SURVIVAL AND THE SHIFTING FRONTIER

Nowhere is the independence and self-sufficiency standard for individual behavior more evident than in our perceptions of those historical periods where the frontiers of the New World were being opened. These perceptions have considerable basis in fact. One cannot stand on any piece of American real estate and contemplate what life must have been like for the first settlers without being struck by the incredible hardships which had to be faced and overcome. Stand, for example, on the deck of the Mayflower replica and try to imagine what possible desperation with an existing life situation or vision of a better one compelled the Pilgrims to cram themselves into that tiny vessel and set out across the ocean. Travel through Kansas on an interstate highway in an air-conditioned car and contrast that with a journey over the prairie by covered wagon. Were those the good old days?

On a frontier, whether that frontier was in New England, Missouri, Louisiana or the far reaches of the Northwest, survival was the basic human welfare issue. Suffering and hardship were virtually universal. Meeting basic needs for food, clothing, shelter and defense required the full energies of everyone. Unpleasant as such a lifestyle may be, managing to survive in a harsh physical environment can give those who make it an immediate sense of having achieved substantial control over their own destinies, though they might also have to acknowledge that they had been lucky or blessed in having been spared death from obstacles beyond their individual control such as illness, drought, and flood. The survival lifestyle seemed to prove that with a lot of individual determination and luck, people could shape their own lives without interference from the state and other human social creations.

Though it is true that first settlers on any frontier are not "burdened" by the presence of familiar institutions and organizational structures, it is imperative to remember that they do not create new ones completely from scratch. First settlers bring a legal and religious heritage and some basic artifacts which reflect existing commerce and technology. They are also the beneficiaries as well as the victims of active institutional intervention.

In the colonial period, for example, oppressive government and religious policies as well as economic conditions inspired or, in the case of slaves and transported convicts, coerced individuals to seek life on the new continent. The exodus from the mother countries served those national interests by getting rid of misfits and malcontents while expanding the nation's economic and political strength. Governments controlled or tried to control who got what land and business through such mechanisms as chartering trade companies, giving land grants, establishing military control, and appointing civil officials to act in the name of the Crown.

As the frontier moved westward, the personal inclinations of hardy individuals to escape old obligations or to strike out for new opportunities were again encouraged by active government policy, this time of the young American government. Wars over territory, land acquisitions such as the Louisiana Purchase, and laws such as the Homestead Act of 1862 are examples of institutional support for what was perceived as individual accomplishment. The concept of manifest destiny was clearly in vogue and served a useful social purpose both for a developing nation and for that portion of its population which was desperate, restless, greedy, anti-social or just plain curious enough to risk finding out what lay over the next river or mountain range. Yet, regardless of how they perceived it, the pioneers did not make it entirely on their own.

Some of the hardy, individualistic pioneers were loners who did not want to be entangled with other people. Most, however, came in groups or at least settled in clusters and began to experience a sense of community and of relationship to neighbors even where "next door" was miles away. It took little imagination to see that chances for survival could be increased and life in general made a little less harrowing by a certain amount of cooperation and involvement with others. Besides, it was easy to understand your neighbor's predicament because it was yours too; it was easy to make your own judgment about the causes of his misfortune. The mutual self-help neighborly activities which took place in the early settlements provided economic and sometimes recreational benefits to all involved, and they did constitute volunteer work in a rudimentary sense.

War in any era is a special case of the survival phenomenon in terms of its relationship to volunteering. Here again the necessity of cooperative effort for survival is clear and the level of expectation for all citizens' participation in the survival effort is higher than normal. Extraordinary demands require and inspire extraordinary response. For peace groups and conscientious objectors, war also becomes the occasion for extraordinary hostility.

2.3 THE DEVELOPMENT OF COMMUNITY--AGRARIAN STYLE

As settlements grew and some of the roughest edges of the physical environment had been smoothed down, citizens in more established areas began to recognize that their proximity created new concerns which could not be addressed without additional cooperation. These concerns included: fire protection, public safety, epidemic control, building and maintenance of roads and bridges, water, and sanitation. The clearest way to

meet these needs at first was for individuals to pitch
in and do whatever had to be done. This included
contributions of materials as well as of time, energy,
and brute strength. When money was also required,
door-to-door solicitations and lotteries became customary. Emerging town governments were staffed by
citizen volunteers who assumed community management
responsibilities and concomitant prestige as selectmen,
surveyors, clerks of the market, town criers, and the
like.

The development of community maintenance services
of this nature followed an evolutionary pattern. Citizens as a group recognized the need and through
voluntary effort provided the service. As demand for
the service increased, responsibility for its provision
was placed with the elected local government and
eventually became tax supported. The timing by which
this pattern unfolded varied with each service and with
the stage of development in a given geographic
area. However, the significant point is that these
services, by and large, were viewed as essential by a
large enough segment of the population that they tended
to evoke relatively minimal controversy. The debates
were more apt to have been on how to rather than whether
to provide them.

There is one tidbit related to this pattern which
appears in the history books as a semi-amusing aside but
which bears on the status of volunteering today. As it
turns out, one of the factors contributing to the
transfer of firefighting from volunteers to public
employees was the sheer rowdiness and unreliability of
many volunteer fire companies. Fighting fires was and
is dangerous work. Citizens who chose to do it were
greatly respected by their fellow citizens. The promise
of prestige ultimately produced a less than healthy
competition among fire companies. In the absence of
adequate definitions of geographic jurisdiction, the
companies often raced each other to the scene and
literally fought over who would put out the fire. Needless to say, valuable time was lost by such behavior. Also the exploits of some volunteer posses and
vigilante groups have been cause for community examination of how best to assure law and order in a legal and
orderly fashion.

Economic dependency was another community maintenance concern identified early more as a threat to the common good than as a matter of common decency. This was certainly not an issue born on American soil. However, in a free country whose economy was tied to a particularly promising land, it was easy to be suspicious of those persons who could not achieve minimal subsistence by their own labors. Prevailing religious beliefs confirmed that economic failure was moral failure but also taught that good folks had an obligation to help the less fortunate.

To the extent possible, families took care of their own aged, infirm or unlucky. Local governments were expected to control the influx of dependents and did so with such mechanisms as appointing volunteer overseers of the poor, "warning out" newcomers with no clear means of support, billing each other for services rendered to dependents who had come from another place, and requiring citizens to report if they were keeping long-term "guests" in their homes. Widows were helped to find gainful employment; orphans and illegitimate children were apprenticed or taken in by foster families. The assistance provided by the community at large ranged from sensitive and caring to abusive and exploitative. Eventually the numbers of persons unable to care for themselves became large enough that institutions were established. At first these were generalized almshouses and workhouses where all of the community's left overs were placed. Only later did they become more specialized to deal with different causes of dependency.

In addition to individual acts of charity and minimal grudging actions of local governments, citizens concerned with the poor made use of another tool for addressing the problems they saw: the much-heralded voluntary association. The purposes of some of these groups are evident in their names: Society for the Relief of Distressed Debtors, Society for the Relief of Poor Widows with Small Children, Association for Improving the Condition of the Poor, and Society for Alleviating the Miseries of Public Prisons. Early labor organizations began as benevolent societies concerned with the sick, disabled, widowed, and orphaned among their number. Much of the activity was aimed at providing direct service to those in need such as collecting clothing, setting up soup kitchens, running orphan asylums, and lecturing on the evils of drink and other obstacles to self-reliance. This direct service was supported by fundraising and other organizational maintenance activities, and there were organizers and officers responsible for policy making.

So vast were the good intentions and so numerous were the resulting efforts that, by the early nineteenth century, still other volunteers began to believe that part of the dependency problem was ill-regulated, indiscriminate charity. Groups like the Society for the Prevention of Pauperism in the City of New York were formed to address this concern, thereby perhaps becoming one of the first groups to assert that meaning well is not enough. Another philosophy whose good intentions ultimately backfired was the Quaker belief that solitary confinement was the road to prisoner rehabilitation. Later prison reformers felt that this had done more harm than good.

These kinds of responses to need were made possible not only by the charitable instincts of individuals but also by the relative availability of leisure time and discretionary income enjoyed by at least some segments of society. These responses resulted from the stabilizing of the physical environment, the success of agriculture, and the continuing growth of commerce and trade.

Such relative comfort also allowed for the rise of other quality-of-life concerns. Churches had long been a top priority and were built by cooperative effort early in the development of community life. Colleges and seminaries were among the early institutions founded by private philanthropic effort. Those who valued education for the young built school houses and hired teachers where possible. If this were not feasible, volunteer teachers were recruited. The more well-to-do had the time and resources to promote the development of libraries and museums whose purposes were to share with the general public those cultural resources which had formerly been the province of royalty. Hospitals and dispensaries slowly came into being through voluntary effort as resources and medical knowledge increased. Basically, for every cause one could think of, there was a voluntary association created to deal with it.

It is tempting to romanticize this volunteer spirit and to assume that once the volunteers started a social ball rolling, its appeal was irresistible, its acceptance universally desired, and its implementation only a matter of time. This was not necessarily so. For example, at this point, education was definitely optional at extra cost. While the Puritan ideal of public education as essential to the public good was alive in the abstract, some of the tough issues such as tax support and compulsory attendance were yet to come. Dispensaries were established in response to middle class demand that medical care which was available privately to the rich and at public expense to the poor be accessible to them too. The idea of culture as a public trust is still struggling for acceptance. In other words, the question of how much of the good life belongs to whom and at whose expense has always been debated.

The intended consequences of many of these efforts was to extend opportunities and services to a wider cross section of the community than would have had access to them under the rigid Old World class sytem. However, this has not necessarily meant to all Americans. For the most part, concepts of human dignity, human welfare, and social justice applied at first only to free white men and almost exclusively to protestant Christian ones. If one perceives of Indians as savages, blacks as chattel equal to three-fifths of a person, and women and children as property, there are a lot of issues which simply do not come to the forefront of one's thinking. With all the demands of forging a new society even for free white men, it is at least understandable, if not laudable, that our forefathers were egalitarian only to a point.

An unintended consequence of the democratic ideal as promoted by the original settlers has been that some persons and groups have always disagreed with the prevailing sentiment. They have believed that the pursuit of liberty and happiness included all humans, not just those whom law and custom defined as persons at that moment; and they have actively promoted their version of equality and justice. However, shared opposition to current opinion and practice has not automatically produced agreement among dissenters on how to correct the perceived injustice. The well-known social reform movements such as abolition, women's rights, and labor which came to full flower in the nineteenth century were never single-visioned, monolithic entities driven by the righteousness of The Cause and moving inexorably toward The Goal.

For example, many citizens opposed the abolition of slavery but did feel that one should treat slaves humanely, in much the same way we now speak of being humane to animals. Some reformers advocated abolition followed by sending freed blacks to African colonies. The Colonization Societies received the support of Southern plantation owners who were not anxious to end slavery but were very interested in removing freed blacks from the sight of slaves. Freed blacks opposed colonization and organized to fight vigorously for the right to stay in America and obtain the privileges of citizenship.

As the abolition movement gained strength in the pre-Civil War era, there were power struggles for leadership such as the major one between Garrison and Douglass. There were knotty issues, such as what to do about women and women's rights, which raised complex questions of strategy and tactics for would-be reformers. The hazards of a pro-abolition stance were, of course, not exclusively internal. Anti-slavery volunteers took considerable personal risk, particularly those who operated the Underground Railroad. Meaning well on this issue proved costly indeed. Similar intricacies characterized the labor and women's movements; these will be explored later.

2.4 MOVING THE WORKPLACE--INDUSTRIALIZATION AND URBANIZATION

As if the challenges of establishing communities in an agriculture-based economy were not enough, some other developments were occurring which dramatically changed the structures of American society. Advances in science and technology fueled by the availability of natural resources and sparked by the creative genius of now-famous scientists and inventors found a receptive market among the American public eager to improve its standard of living and to benefit from the goods which could be produced by machines. The manufacturing of items heretofore hand-wrought or unavailable altogether offered a promise of a better, easier life than previously imaginable. New stock on store shelves and widespread use of mail-order catalogs brought the promise of the good life to all the citizenry, and considerable public favor was bestowed on nearly all efforts of promoting industrialism.

The prospect of new sources of wealth inspired entrepreneurial and investment activity of an unprecedented magnitude. The rapid expansion of manufacturing was supported by the gradual development of business corporation laws which defined the entity, limited the liability of individual investors, gave "personhood" and concomitant individual rights to such bodies under the Fourteenth Amendment, and had the effect of giving virtually free reign to the pioneers on this new frontier. It also produced a new class of community leader and power broker: the industrialist.

The prospect of a better life, if not necessarily great wealth, attracted workers to the new workplace--factories. Leaving the isolation and hardship of the farms, many Americans moved to the growing cities seeking new fortunes. Immigrants continued to flood in largely from Europe but also from Asia with hopes of building a new life in the land of freedom and opportunity. The realities which awaited these native and foreign-born workers were long hours, unsafe working conditions, poor pay, no benefits, inadequate housing and other hardships. In addition they had forfeited the option of eking out a subsistence on the land and were at the mercy of the factory owners' benevolence or lack of it. Industrial paternalism shaped many a community and became a pattern which later proved to be hard to break even when its problems became evident.

As much as the mushrooming industrial economy needed the large unskilled labor pool which seemed eager and willing, no one was prepared to deal adequately with the problems caused by relocating the nation's primary workplace from the farm to the factory and from the countryside to rapidly expanding cities and towns. Urban poverty was physically concentrated and

29

highly visible. Squalor, disease, and crime took on new and unglorious dimensions in the more centralized setting. The fact that many of this new labor pool were non-English-speaking, non-Protestant, and/or nonwhite further compounded an already difficult situation. The Irish, Chinese, Eastern Europeans, Japanese and emancipated American blacks were far from welcomed with open arms in their efforts to share the American dream.

There were citizens who found the living and working conditions of the urban poor appalling and who felt that something had to be done to improve those conditions. Many states had established Boards of Charities to oversee such relief efforts as were going on. Voluntary associations blossomed to provide services, among them YMCA's, YWCA's, YMHA's, YWHA's, Salvation Army, Children's Aid Societies, and settlement houses. Charity Organization Societies were formed to dispense charity in a more "scientific" or at least disciplined way. Volunteers served as friendly visitors whose function was to establish the worthiness of each case and to dispense advice to the needy. One thing all of this voluntary activity seemed to have in common was the perception that the answer to the needy persons' problems was to imbue them with the ideals and lifestyles of white Anglo-Saxon society. The programs of these groups "did for" and "acted in the best interests of" the needy and established a pattern of welfare paternalism which was later adopted by government.

Workers themselves gradually expressed objections to their treatment by moving beyond mutual self-help benevolent societies into increasingly militant labor organizations. Like the abolition movement, the "labor movement" encompassed a wide variety of activities and groups which were often at odds with each other as well as with the powerful entrepreneurial class. Skilled craft unions, after making use of strikes, resented the intrusion of unskilled workers onto this turf which they had established. Some unions were very restrictive in membership; other groups sought broad-based labor representation. Some groups incorporated a wide range of social and economic issues into their philosophies; others kept to strictly workplace-related concerns. It took a century of struggle for organized labor to achieve a position of power. This struggle and its current manifestations were to have serious consequences for volunteering which will be explored later.

Other quality-of-life issues abounded. Supporters of public education continued the struggle for improving the quality and quantity of schooling available to the general population, the high school and kindergarten movements being examples. Colleges and universities proliferated thanks largely to private philanthropic efforts and local civic pride but thanks also to the growing commitment of state and federal government. Museums and libraries grew in numbers generally with the initial push and major funding coming from private groups but often in active partnership with government bodies which sometimes donated land and gave tax support for operations as well as granting the enabling charters.

Looking again at the workplace for a moment, there was a revolution other than unionization going on: professionalization. The struggles here were quieter, but they were to have a profound, negative impact on the status of volunteers. At this point in history, however, they represented progress of a substantial sort. Certain occupations, notably medicine, law, and the ministry, had long been perceived as requiring special education and training and carrying with them certain ethical obligations for their practitioners. These occupations dealt with areas of life where any problems were crucial and solutions to them were perceived to require an expertise not generally available to ordinary folk. Standards for required education and definitions of competent practice fluctuated widely at different points in history. However, these professions had had an early start on building credibility, trust, and, in the case of doctors and lawyers, financial reward. Advances in medical science and the ever-increasing complexity of the law supported the case for the accreditation of training institutions and the establishment of stiff entrance requirements for would-be doctors and lawyers.

Hoping to follow the pattern of professional practice and prestige started in medicine and law, workers in other service areas began to clamor for professional recognition. Nurses, teachers, and librarians, for example, worked hard to promote their fields as distinct disciplines worthy of the profession label. Social work was a brand new field which grew out of the experience gained by friendly visitors and other social welfare volunteers and out of the growing body of knowledge being offered by the new academic disciplines of sociology and psychology. For the most part, the increased demand for services in these fields was the result of volunteer accomplishments in demonstrating need, introducing methodologies, and discovering the limits of volunteer involvement. Professionalization was also occurring in government where competency-based civil service was introduced as an alternative to the prevailing system of political appointment which invited incompetence, graft, and corruption.

The road to professionalism proved to be very rocky for reasons which will be explored in the next two chapters. For now, however, try to imagine the pride a volunteer organization must have felt when it achieved sufficient sophistication and solvency to be able to hire its first executive secretary. Share the pride of a citizens' reform group which watched a government department become staffed with trained personnel instead of a party boss's lackeys.

2.5 CLOSING THE FRONTIER

The physical expansion of the national domain to encompass the full width of the continent was virtually completed by the end of the nineteenth century. In a sense, the frontier was closed. However, the continued expansion of science and industry kept the sense of manifest destiny and its related perceptions of opportunity and optimism alive. When the limits of the domestic market fell short of the production capacity of industry, new markets were found in foreign countries. The American government gave its moral and military support to such expansion, and the nation became more visibly entangled with other nations. At home, new wonders of technology were continuously introduced to the general public. Electric lights, telephones, radios, cars, moving pictures and countless other mind-boggling innovations added to the belief that only in America could such miracles take place. The sky remained the limit, a perception which even the disruption caused by world wars and foreign skirmishes seemed only to confirm.

In the realm of volunteerism, activity flourished as assorted interest groups and organizations plugged away at the needs they perceived as urgent. Boy's Clubs, Boy and Girl Scouts, Campfire Girls, 4-H Clubs and family service/child welfare organizations joined the ranks of established service groups. Scientific charity was made more businesslike as well with the advent of federated fundraising by community chests. Charity as a socially acceptable activity gained credibility with the birth of Rotary, Kiwanis, and similar community service clubs for businessmen. Junior Leagues and Women's Clubs provided a comparable outlet for women of leisure. Groups like the NAACP, the Urban League, and the League of Women Voters promoted their respective social justice causes. Apparently there was still much to be done in realizing the American dream and many citizens willing to try to make it happen.

In all areas of social and economic concern, there was a steadily increasing amount of activity taking place in government particularly at the Federal level. When public or private voluntary attempts to correct a problem did not result in solutions at local and state levels, answers were sought in Federal laws, agencies, and courts. Government had begun to move against the most blatant abuses of rampant capitalism and was more and more perceived as the arena in which individual and community interests could be reconciled most equitably. The enthusiastic reformers known as Progressives gained considerable support for viewing the state as a benevolent parent. Advocates against child labor and for compulsory school attendance, against unsafe working conditions and for workmen's compensation had more and more successes. Progressive reforms such as the establishment of juvenile courts and the introduction of probation and widows' pension programs set the stage for the transfer of welfare paternalism from private to public hands; this shift dramatically occurred during the Great Depression of the 1930's.

2.6 OUR VOLUNTEER HERITAGE

This cursory review of substantive topics barely scratches the surface of the wide-ranging activities involving volunteers during the agrarian and industrial eras. It certainly does justice to no single issue mentioned and omits several that some would believe to be important or interesting. If it seems disjointed, that is at least partially because these were times of unbridled volunteerism. It does, however, suggest several themes about American volunteering which carry over to modern times.

(a) The sense of open-endedness and manifest destiny which characterized the frontier mentality and was augmented by the grand promise of science and industry seemed to place no limit on the heights individuals could expect to achieve and on the breadth of opportunities society could provide those individuals.

(b) Volunteer-type citizens extrapolated the rights of individuals to pursue life, liberty and happiness to include the right to turn an individual concern into a public issue and work at it until one succeeded or got tired, with little or no obligation to worry about unintended consequences let alone planning and co-ordination.

(c) The one-to-one, neighbor-helping-neighbor model of "meaning well" was not enough to resolve all the social concerns that citizens experienced. Achieving the desired results usually required banding together with like-minded individuals and organizing in some fashion. As issues changed, some groups died, and new ones took their place. Or old ones adapted to the new tasks, though some no doubt stayed alive in form if not substance beyond the relevance of their efforts to the problems at hand.

(d) Expediency was the name of the game. Even within the range of legal means, many options existed for resolving various concerns: promoting public awareness, providing services by private effort, cajoling and lobbying at whatever level of government seemed most responsive, and assorted combinations of all these. Expediency also required accepting support from wherever it could be gotten without too much concern about the ramifications of hidden agendas. In addition to the example of plantation owner support of colonization cited above, there were other illustrations of this. For instance, the development of public high schools was supported by the middle classes who wanted to move one step closer to the privately-educated gentry and to keep one step ahead of the riff-raff as well as by altruistic promoters of equal educational opportunity. Also it did not hurt the abstract cause of civil service reform that many of the corrupt city leaders were of immigrant stock.

(e) Volunteers opened one Pandora's box after another. The fact that they were attempting to unleash good rather than evil did not preclude disagreement, disharmony, confusion, and frustration. They were successful in varying degrees and did keep many issues alive and kicking.

Ironically their most consistent accomplishment may have been in unleashing forces which would later turn on them. With the seeds for unionization, professionalization, bureaucratization, big government, and client resistance sown by their efforts, volunteers were on their way to becoming unloved stepchildren simply by virtue of being volunteers.

How this affects volunteerism in the modern era is a theme we will resume in Chapter 4 after we look at another historical development: the legacy of Lady Bountiful.

RESOURCES

Allen, Robert. RELUCTANT REFORMERS: THE IMPACT OF RACISM ON AMERICAN SOCIAL REFORM MOVEMENTS. Washington, D.C.: Howard University Press, 1974.

Bakal, Carl. CHARITY USA. New York: Times Books, 1979.

Church, Robert L. EDUCATION IN THE UNITED STATES: AN INTERPRETIVE HISTORY. New York: The Free Press, 1976.

Ellis, Susan J. and Noyes, Katherine H. BY THE
     PEOPLE: A HISTORY OF AMERICANS AS VOLUN-
     TEERS. Philadelphia: ENERGIZE, 1978.

Friedman, Lawrence M. A HISTORY OF AMERICAN LAW. New
     York: Simon and Schuster, 1973.

Furnas, J.C. THE AMERICANS: A SOCIAL HISTORY OF THE
     UNITED STATES 1587-1914. New York: G. P. Putnam's
     Sons, 1969.

Gaylin, Willard; Glasser, Ira; Marcus, Steven; and
     Rothman, David. DOING GOOD: THE LIMITS OF BENE-
     VOLENCE. New York: Pantheon Books, 1978.

Katz, Herbert and Katz, Marjorie. MUSEUMS, U.S.A.: A
     HISTORY AND GUIDE. Garden City, NY: Doubleday and
     Co., Inc., 1965.

Schwartz, Bernard. THE LAW IN AMERICA: A HISTORY. New
     York: McGraw-Hill Book Co., 1974.

3

THE LEGACY OF LADY BOUNTIFUL

3.1 A CURIOUS CONTRADICTION

From any review of volunteers in American history, even one as cursory as that in Chapter 2, it is readily apparent that volunteers have always come from both sexes, all races, all economic classes, and a full· range of philosophical persuasions. The subject matter of volunteer efforts has impinged directly on nearly every organization and institution in our society, and the type of activities has been very diverse depending on the demands of the situation. It appears that, for the most part, volunteers did what they deemed prudent without much concern for their status as volunteers. Hence it is relatively easy to understand that to some degree society's perception of the value of volunteers has been influenced by the content of the volunteer's cause and the methods used to promote it. That evaluation has ranged from anathema to admiration based on the subject matter of volunteer effort.

While this is an important historical component of modern ideas about volunteering's place in society, it does not explain the curious contradiction which has arisen with regard to the status of volunteers today. The contradiction is this: The facts indicate that large numbers and great varieties of Americans engage in all kinds of volunteer work. Yet somehow the word "volunteer" has come to have a very narrow application which evokes an image of well-to-do women, who have nothing better to do, running around supposedly doing good works. Furthermore the word "volunteer" has acquired a connotation of extraneousness to the real world which applies to both the volunteer and the volunteer work being done.

This very limited and limiting picture of volunteers has taken on a life of its own and has itself become one of the facts with which modern volunteers and students of volunteering must deal, even though it blatantly conflicts with the other kinds of evidence available about the nature and scope of volunteering.

This reduction of the volunteer image is most commonly expressed in glib references to Lady Bountiful, that rich lady who once in a while put on her hat and gloves and personally delivered a food basket to the needy family on the other side of town. The food was, of course, bought with her husband's hard-earned money and was prepared and packed by her cook. The recipients of her largesse may or may not have had enough food to eat between her sporadic visits. However, she meant well. And wasn't she nice doing her Christian duty like that?

In this seemingly clear and simple mental picture are a number of clues about the nature of volunteers and volunteering which, with the exception of gender, have largely been ignored. The Lady Bountiful stereotype has its origins in certain historical realities of nineteenth-century lifestyles and has given a legacy to the twentieth century whose net effect might be termed the feminization of volunteering.

3.2 EATING BREAD AND HONEY

To begin with, Lady Bountiful was a lady in the Victorian sense of the word. She belonged to the ever increasing upper-middle and upper classes whose levels of affluence and subsequent comfort resulted from being on the right end of the Industrial Revolution. She was generally the wife of a successful business or profes- sional man, although sometimes she was an unmarried female relative dependent on said gentleman. In either case, she lived in and largely enjoyed a degree of comfort unthinkable to her pioneer ancestors and to large numbers of her contemporaries in the working classes. Her lifestyle was reminiscent of the nursery rhyme queen who could be found in the parlor eating bread and honey.

As a proper Victorian wife, she was in charge of supervising a household which was staffed to varying degrees by paid servants. She often had help with child care from nurses, governesses, or tutors. Since her husband's work and many of his social activities kept him away from home much of the time, she was left to her own devices to pursue activities of her own choosing so long as they were considered proper. In all things she was expected to reflect her husband's achievements by proper attire and decorum, by respectable social activities in acceptable circles of people, and by keeping her nose out of matters that did not affect her home and family. Her presumed delicacy and her very idleness were important status symbols in an era which cannonized virtuous and vacuous womanhood.

However, "ladies" were still female in the legal and economic as well as the obvious sense. In the nineteenth century, this meant having no voting rights, very limited political clout, no substantial rights to her own property, and limited access to the work- place. Lady Bountiful did have the advantages of not needing access to the workplace and of having pin money, if her husband chose to dole it out. These remained advantages as long as her husband was in fact successful and did choose to support her in the style to which most people would like to become accustomed.

However, she was learning first hand that large amounts of ease and leisure time can be burdensome and that a Cinderella existence has its limitations. After all, if you are dancing backwards through life in glass slippers, you need to make sure that your partner does not step on your toes. Lady Bountiful faced a real challenge in filling her days with activities which were socially acceptable and at the same time met some of her personal needs, not the least of which may have been for feelings of usefulness and companionship.

"Ladies" had several options. They could capitalize on delicateness by succumbing to "the vapors," a very real though nonspecific chronic condition characterized by nervousness and depression. A lady might also have very real health problems, for even affluent women could not avoid tuberculosis, cancer, and problems resulting from frequent child-bearing, given the status of medical knowledge and the prevailing custom of women not openly discussing their bodies with anyone including doctors. Closed-in houses filled with the fumes of burning wood or coal and fashions which required corseting and the wearing of up to twelve pounds of clothing further taxed the physical well-being of all but the most robust. If the truth were known, these burdensome fashions probably encouraged the queen to restrict her intake of bread and honey. In any event, illness, whether feigned or real, justified inactivity.

Other leisure time options available to ladies included needlework, music, and reading novels. All of these were extensions of the finishing school approach to education and self-development considered in many circles to be adequate for well-bred young women. Social functions with elaborate rituals and strict protocol occupied considerable time. To the twentieth-century mind perhaps the quaintest example of these pastimes was the widespread practice of "calling" or being "at home" to receive callers and of making judicious use of calling cards. That such old customs die slowly was brought home to this writer when, in the mid-1960's, she met a new bride who had received a dozen monogrammed calling card trays as wedding gifts and not a single toaster.

3.3   BEYOND THE PARLOR

Ladies were permitted to participate in some other kinds of activities outside the parlors of their homes. Church work had long been an acceptable outlet for women's energies even before Lady Bountiful came on the scene as a distinct force. For women, church work meant sitting together, often in the church parlors, sewing articles for missionaries to use for themselves or among those distant folk they were trying to convert. It meant running bazaars and fairs to raise money for religious causes identified as legitimate by the male church leadership and keeping the altar linens and communion silver in top condition. Charity work through the many voluntary associations which were proliferating was an acceptably ladylike extension of neighboring and church work. Hence in these areas Lady Bountiful was carrying on a fairly long-standing tradition.

Club work became an important outlet for women in the late nineteenth century. Having tasted responsibilities outside the home during the Civil War and aware of, if not active in, developments in higher education for women, ladies sought companionship and intellectual stimulation in the rapidly growing women's clubs, many of which eventually affiliated under the General Federation of Women's Clubs. Provocative informational programs and the heady experience of fellowship led many club women into public policy areas and community service work as individuals and in groups. There they could put the leadership and organizational skills they had learned within their club structure to work on what they perceived to be meaningful social issues.

Perhaps one of the greatest ironies in the history of women as volunteers is that they were by their actions saying that women have a place in the community other than home and yet were often doing things which, from the vantage point of the twentieth century, appear to have reinforced their second-class status. The tools and strategies available to civic-minded women were constrained by the conventions associated with being a lady. The resulting limitations may not have been widely recognized since most women accepted the beliefs of the day that women were properly subordinate to men.

For example, direct service charity work could be justified as an expression of woman's "natural" instincts for nurturing and for tending to the needs of others. It also was an extension of her homemaking skills to serve the community at large. There was a place for women in organizational structures but often as the group's housekeeper providing refreshments, building on pin money to raise funds for the "real" work of the association, and doing odds and ends as they came up.

This auxiliary mentality seemed so natural that the ladies of Boston who raised large sums of money on behalf of the blind might still feel it appropriate that history gives the credit to Samuel Gridley Howe, whose vision and leadership gave birth to schools for the blind. That intrepid crusader, Dorothea Dix, was widely known and admired for her efforts to improve treatment of the mentally ill. Yet even she sometimes found it more politic to send her concerns and suggestions for action through sympathetic male legislators than to present them herself. The early advocates for women's suffrage, who are not by the way part of the Lady Bountiful stereotype, saw or were forced to see that their concerns would have to take a back seat until the question of black male suffrage was resolved.

Ladies were also permitted to use feminine wiles in order to further their causes, within the bounds of decency of course. A case in point was the so-called "pout and sulk" approach in which women engaged to show their support for the Civil War effort. If a male relative or acquaintance seemed reluctant to enlist as a soldier, a lady could wave a petticoat under his nose and suggest that he might wear it. She might also deny him access to her attentions.

While pouting and sulking, wheedling and cajoling might get a job done, it has the effect of minimizing the abilities and accomplishments of the women them- selves. The petticoat wavers proved to be hardy souls. They shouldered full home and business responsibilities while their men were at war. They also did much of the nursing, sewing of uniforms, amassing and distributing of supplies, and other duties critical to the war effort. When some of these activities were organized under the United States Sanitary Commission, women raised fifty million dollars to support its work, no small amount by any standard and certainly an impressive one for the holders of pin money. The postwar return to normalcy was understandably welcome, but it did include women resuming their roles as sweet, dependent, empty-headed personages at least for a time.

As a rule, most public speaking and virtually all political activity were deemed unladylike. Yet there were some exceptions. When the cause could be interpreted as promoting the sanctity of the home or of womanhood, social action and advocacy by women was tolerated. Temperance, child health, education, hygiene, and anti-women's suffrage fell in this category. The suffragists made use of this by comparing the untenable status of white womanhood with the enfranchised position of blacks and immigrants, when the case for women's voting rights did not sell on its own merits.

Finally many of the activities associated more exclusively with Lady Bountiful may have accomplished useful short-term results but created long-term consequences which have fallen to later generations to address. The relationship of charity as a contributor to dependency is still a subject for debate, though generally not by those in desperate need of a food basket. Ladies who were genuinely distressed by the physical and moral threats to female virtue they saw in factory work did their best to guide young women into domestic service and clerical work, not knowing they were promoting dead ends in the area of women's employment. Other ladies, aware that even middle-class women could fall on hard times financially but still anxious to preserve the notion that ladies did not work, set up Women's Exchanges where homemade items of food and clothing could be sold and the money discreetly transmitted to the needy woman who had labored quietly in her home to produce the goods.

Many of these observations about Lady Bountiful are made from the comfortable vantage point of hindsight. Yet the stereotype is real and does represent a real historical phenomenon. Is Lady Bountiful to be praised or condemned? Was she courageous or cowardly? She undoubtedly earned any assessment one cares to make, for she represents many different women doing many different things. She is not a replica modeled after a single, named heroine. At the very least she reminds us that enough people acting on their good intentions can have an impact.

3.4 MEANWHILE AT THE COUNTINGHOUSE

Where was Lord Bountiful while Lady Bountiful was so busy and was assuming such large proportions in our image of volunteers? Again the nursery rhyme provides clues about the gentleman and his lifestyle. Though only a king in his own house, Lord Bountiful did belong to the new ruling class: successful businessman. If he did not actually work in a countinghouse, he was, nevertheless, likely to be working in an executive office situation of some kind. He may well have worked long and hard at his business responsibilities, but it was a substantively different kind of long and hard than that of his pioneer ancestors or many of his own employees. He, like Lady Bountiful, no longer had to spend every waking hour just surviving and did have time to pursue other activities.

As a gentleman, he was considerably less constrained in his use of leisure than the women in his life. In his daily business routine he already had access to more peer contact than his wife. He could seek additional companionship in the halls of his club or at meetings of his social organizations. If he wanted to play an active role in community life, he had access to the public forums, voting booths, legislative chambers and back rooms where policies were determined and decisions made. Because his experience in the for-profit corporate world was presumed to carry over into the business end of the not-for-profit organization, he had opportunities to serve on the boards and in leadership roles of voluntary associations. Lord Bountiful also had the option of contributing his money directly to causes he considered worthy, emulating on his own scale the pattern attributed to John D. Rockefeller, Andrew Carnegie and other famous philanthropists. If he did any or all of these, he perceived himself and was perceived as doing the civic duty befitting his position.

Yet perhaps he too was restricted in acting on his social concerns by the prevailing definitions of ladies and gentlemen and the distinct spheres of socially acceptable endeavors associated with those definitions. It would have been unseemly for a gentleman of his station to deliver food baskets or to visit the sick and elderly, regardless of how effective he might have been at that or how much personal satisfaction he might have gained from such direct, hands-on experience. Such possibilities probably did not even occur to him. If he were not interested in politics or was not enamored with board or committee work, any charitable inclinations he might have could be taken care of by a contribution or gestures of support for Lady Bountiful's efforts.

That men participated in volunteer work is a fact. That their participation was frequently not called volunteer work and that there is no Lord Bountiful stereotype comparable to the Lady Bountiful one is significant and is better understood in light of two other components of the stereotype which are not overtly gender related.

3.5 LEISURE TIME AS PLAYTIME

Leisure time is a phrase which creeps into any discussion of volunteering. Leisure time was a scarce resource on the frontiers and remained so for many groups of workers and their families on the farms and in the factories. In sharp contrast, the upper classes had considerably more of it, Lady Bountiful and her friends personifying the ultimate in leisurely living conceivable in a democratic society.

By definition leisure is what one has when not working. Work is generally considered to be that set of activities by which one earns a livelihood. In that framework, it contrasts with play so that activities

45

conducted when one is not earning one's living are construed to be recreational. This straightforward work/play dichotomy may be accurate for categorizing the major activities of those who have to be on the job for long, hard hours and who, with but a small amount of time and energy left over, choose to relax over a beer or at a hoedown or some other form of just plain fun. That there could be a dichotomy at all represents a change from the days when spare time was so scarce that even children did not play much and adult socializing took place primarily around events whose main purpose was to accomplish essential work. The dichotomy is not useful, however, in understanding the impact of large amounts of leisure time on people like the Bountifuls.

In other contexts, the word "work" was often preceded by an adjective which presumably refined its meaning. Farm work, factory work, office work, man's work, woman's work, civic work, charity work, club work and church work are some distinctions relevant to the Bountifuls' era which we have already encountered. All of these variations on the theme imply that time and energy are being applied to specified tasks for which the worker is accountable. However, "real" work remained that which one did for money or survival. Leisure was that desirable, amorphous commodity with which one could do what pleased his or her fancy. The most that could be said for any gray areas of activity was that they were busy work.

Thus it was Lady Bountiful whose image most felt the impact of these definitions. She was already freed from most of that portion of women's duties which would have been called real work. Much of her time was spent planning and participating in social events which may have felt like work to her and were in fact part of her job as wife but which smacked of playing to the average citizen. She had attained or, depending on your point of view, been forced into a position of irrelevance to the workplace, i.e., the "real" world. Her distance from this world was further increased as some fields in which she had labored, specifically social work, nursing, and teaching, became "reality" by virtue of having paid staff in new professional fields assume many of the duties which had previously been performed by volunteers.

46

As has already been suggested, when Lady Bountiful ventured into community service activities, she raised questions about which the general society was at best ambivalent. Nonetheless, she persisted. Was she working, playing, pretending to work, dabbling? Did it matter if it was busy work? It somehow seemed simpler to write off all leisure time activities as play and move on to more pressing concerns.

3.6   THE ENIGMA OF NOBLESSE OBLIGE

The final component of the Bountiful image which deserves consideration applied to both the lord and the lady. They exemplified an age-old phenomenon called noblesse oblige which in its simplest form means that the "haves" must behave responsibly toward the "have-nots." Definitions of what constituted responsible behavior could vary substantially, but an even more fundamental question is why? Why should they and why do they?

Both Bountifuls may well have found their motives questioned by their contemporaries. Not every member of their own social class shared their belief that charity work, club work, and civic work were obvious obligations for the well-to-do. Was there some real reason why the needy could not pull themselves up by their own bootstraps? What good could come from all this meddling with the natural selection of the fittest? Isn't politics a pretty dirty business? Besides, what is really in all this activity for the do-gooders?

One can speculate that the Bountifuls acted out of a sense of guilt or at least embarrassment when they compared their comfortable lot with that of the down-and-out and that their good works provided a way to ease their consciences for any role their own success had played in creating such sorry conditions. One can speculate that the Bountifuls were really trying to protect their prestigious position by appeasing the needy with hit-and-miss charity. It could be that the Bountifuls were just plain crazy. Conversely, do-gooders can speculate that it was the noninvolved who felt guilty.

Recipients of the Bountifuls' largesse probably had mixed feelings about their benefactors. Glad as the needy may have been to receive the clothes, food and other assistance offered, they may well have said thank you through clenched teeth, since the help was often accompanied by much unsolicited advice about improving one's life and character. After all, what did the Bountifuls, particularly the lady, know about being poor or having to work for a living? She could dispense relief and advice and then go home to her tea and cookies. She could come back or not, as she chose. In any event, her visits were vivid reminders of the discrepancies in lifestyles and could just as likely evoke resentment as gratitude.

Because the stereotypical Bountifuls were in actuality many different people, it is quite likely that all these suspicions were to some degree based in fact. The Bountifuls may well have been "guilty" of every selfish motivation ascribed to them. They may even have acted intentionally on these grounds. On the other hand, it is also conceivable that they may have acted out of genuine concern, and it is this possibility which creates a discomfort still plaguing volunteerism.

The American dream of individual opportunity presumed that individuals were entitled and could be counted on to pursue life, liberty, and happiness for themselves. What they needed was to be left alone in their pursuit. Persons who felt responsible in some way for the life, liberty, and happiness of others could quickly find themselves out of step with prevailing sentiments about the nature of man, society, and social change. This was particularly true when the problem being addressed seemed to have virtually nothing to do with the volunteer's life situation.

In many areas of volunteer activity, the degree of self-interest is clearer than in the charitable activities attributed particularly to Lady Bountiful. For example, blacks and women in their respective suffrage movements and factory workers who promoted various labor causes could expect a direct, personal benefit if they succeeded. The risks of failure were direct and personal as well. Although sort of one-step-removed, the extraordinary accomplishments of a Harriet Tubman could be explained away since she herself had experienced the injustice she was trying to alleviate. Even Lord Bountiful could be given the "benefit of the doubt" for his involvement. If one did not think the gentleman really cared, one could argue that he was trying to counteract any trace of the cutthroat, robber baron image with which he may have been labeled or that he was simply building good will for business purposes.

People who do good works for no readily apparent reason related to their own self-interest tend to be viewed as curiosities, even threats. Adding the enigma of noblesse oblige to the other issues raised by Lady Bountiful makes for a rather complicated picture. It is easier to perceive her as a curiosity than a threat. It may be safer also, especially if everyone including the lady in question believes that. Besides, she did mean well, and isn't it politer to minimize than to criticize? At least it reduces the risk of upsetting Lord Bountiful.

3.7 THE LEGACY

There is an historical report about a real queen which sums up society's perception of Lady Bountiful as succinctly and accurately as the nursery rhyme describes her lifestyle. Marie Antoinette apparently found being a queen tiresome every now and then. So she would occasionally retire to the Hamlet on the grounds of Versailles. The Hamlet was a working village custom-made to provide the Queen with a firsthand glimpse of how common folk lived. She donned a simple white muslin dress and straw hat and played shepherdess among perfumed sheep until she tired of this diversion and returned to the palace. With this sort of insight into life's realities, it is small wonder that her naive and insensitive if not outrightly malicious solution to the problem of the peasants having no bread was to suggest that they eat cake.

Few people would admit to harboring any such harsh and ludicrous an assessment of Lady Bountiful. Certainly even her staunchest critics would not have wished her the same fate as Marie Antoinette and would have acknowledged that, when Lady Bountiful called on the poor in their homes or visited the wards of public institutions, perfume and sheep were not what she encountered. However, the subtle, steady, and often unintentional devaluation of the lady and her accomplishments has been nearly as devastating as outright condemnation for all volunteers, not just those who are women.

If the word "volunteer" is associated primarily with Lady Bountiful, it is a small step from there to define volunteer work as busy work and to treat it as such. This has resulted in assigning volunteer roles on the basis of sex, regardless of the individual's skills and interests. Furthermore, if the volunteers are presumed to be looking for recreation but an organization needs them to work, it follows that such job-related factors as training, supervision, and accountability for time and productivity must be sugar-coated. If they are expected at all, they surely cannot be required. Besides staff have their "real" jobs to do. If the volunteers are people with time to kill, there is little obligation to worry about making efficient use of their volunteer hours. Since they have pin money, it seems safe to assume that they can absorb any expense associated with their volunteering. The important thing is to keep the good will of the volunteer so that she will speak well of the organization at home and in the community at large. If anything of substance results from her efforts, so much the better.

The Lady Bountiful perception of volunteers and volunteering is very much evident in many contemporary attitudes, policies and practices. It has become fashionable to deny this fervently in defense of The Volunteer or to denounce volunteering because of what Lady Bountiful represents. Rather than assume either extreme posture on the subject right now, let us take a look at some twentieth century trends which have had an impact on volunteering and which need to temper our assessment of whether or not there is anything of value in Lady Bountiful which can be usefully preserved.

RESOURCES

Hahn, Emily. ONCE UPON A PEDESTAL: THE FASCINATING AND INFORMAL CHRONICLE OF THE AMERICAN WOMAN'S STRUGGLE TO STAND ON HER OWN TWO FEET. New York: Thomas Y. Crowell Company, 1974.

Moore, Katharine. VICTORIAN WIVES. New York: St. Martin's Press, 1974.

O'Neill, William L. EVERYONE WAS BRAVE: THE RISE AND FALL OF FEMINISM IN AMERICA. Chicago: Quadrangle Books, 1969.

Rothman, Sheila M. WOMAN'S PROPER PLACE: A HISTORY OF CHANGING IDEALS AND PRACTICES, 1870 TO THE PRESENT. New York: Basic Books, Inc., 1978.

4

NEW WRINKLES, OLD CLOTH

4.1 THE CRAZY QUILT INHERITANCE

To round out our understanding of the historical and social context in which volunteers today are operating, we must now look at the ways in which many of the earlier patterns of volunteer activity have carried over into the late twentieth century in toto or in some vestigial form. Then we can introduce some contemporary wrinkles which have an effect on volunteerism.

As we have seen, these earlier patterns started with recognition of the need to create new structures dealing with community concerns which arose from the making of a new nation. There was widespread belief that citizens left free to pursue their own self-interest and well-being would create those structures in a way which would benefit the community at large. Therefore, they were presumed to have the right to either mind their own business or to promote as a public issue any concern of interest to them using whatever methods seemed to work.

Volunteers forged ahead in community frontiers of their own making, assured that those who disagreed could challenge them, refuse to support their efforts, or, if worse came to worse, leave. Volunteers were confident that somehow progress would result from all this individualistic activity, and they were not entirely wrong in these assumptions. In many instances this is exactly what happened. The result was a crazy-quilt development of services and organizations under public, private, and mixed auspices addressing an endless variety of concerns. New approaches to questions regarding human welfare and dignity were constantly being tested, sometimes succeeding and sometimes found wanting. The needs were so urgent and the options so open that not much attention was paid to the status of the volunteers per se. These issues were more subtle and would, in fact, not come to a head until later.

4.2 THE FRONTIER CLOSES IN

This plethora of volunteer activity reflected the underlying sense of manifest destiny whose mystique retained a powerful hold on the nation's vision of itself long after the physical frontier was closed and well into the 1960's. After all, the country survived the Great Depression of the 1930's, bringing out of that ordeal still another mechanism expressing the nation's concern for and commitment to meeting basic human need. The mechanism this time was in the form of massive Federal intervention in areas of economic and social concern previously viewed as the province of private enterprise, private charity, or local and state government. Whether this change constituted a promising step forward or a giant step toward disaster was and is, of course, a political hot potato. Its significance at this point in our discussion, however, is that it was neither an historical accident nor an historical coup pulled off unilaterally by a charismatic president. It was a rather logical, though admittedly dramatic, extension of the hit-and-miss, do-whatever-works approach to meshing individual human needs, the common good and the national interest. It was another piece of the crazy quilt. If it worked, all would be fine. If it did not, something else could be tried. Or so it seemed.

The next challenge successfully addressed was the massive mobilization of public and private resources to enter and win World War II. The postwar period was marked by impressive economic, scientific and techno-logical growth. The resulting rise in standards of living, best exemplified by rapid growth of suburbs and the idealization of that life style, put the prospect of "the good life" within reach of larger and larger numbers of citizens. Underpinning this atmosphere of growth and rising expectations was the conviction that the nation's natural and social resources were un-limited, that its citizens had unlimited opportunity for upward mobility, and that we were moving inexorably toward a better and better world where everyone could be comfortable and happy.

But some strange things have happened to disrupt this vision. In front of every silver lining is a growing cloud. The same economic and technological growth which made life easier has also made the world smaller and has brought the problems of even the most remote areas into our living rooms. Production of sufficient goods to keep pace with consumer demands has resulted in pollution, a continuing disregard for conservation, and a host of other environmental con-cerns. The suburbs have become a new style of ghetto, and their growth compounds the problems of cities. Advances in medical science mean that people can have healthier and longer lives, but skyrocketing costs and the "graying" of the population present new problems. Large investments of time and money in defense and foreign aid have not created a sense of national security and world peace. Large investments of time and money in social programs have not solved the problems they were set up to address. Poverty, crime, discrimination, unemployment, mental and physical ill-ness, family disintegration and the like continue to be significant and seem virtually insurmountable. However, now we not only have the problems we have big government, big business, big labor and a complex system of established services which seem so mired in their own traditions, bureaucracies and methods of operation that they have become part of the problem.

As the energy crisis and inflation joined the list of problems with full force, the frontier as a national vision closed in, almost snapping shut. This slamming of the door has produced a widespread distrust of established authority and, among many, a sense of powerlessness. It has also generated a reevaluation of methods for fulfilling the American dream and a new thrust or two in voluntary activity.

4.3 ANTI-ESTABLISHMENT VOLUNTEERING

Individual citizens respond differently to the closing of the frontier. Some turn inward and experiment with numerous philosophies and techniques designed to promote self-awareness, self-fulfillment, self-advancement and healthier interpersonal relationships. In these areas of life it is easier to visualize having a chance at controlling and improving one's situation. It has the additional effect of excusing one from involvement with the community and its systems. Others, including large numbers of volunteers already involved with established organizations, believe that the existing systems can be made more responsive and effective if we all work harder and faster and invest more dollars.

Still others, fed up with the way things work and convinced that all will not come to those who wait, have begun actively and angrily challenging the status quo, strengthening their group identity, and demanding their rights. Numbers of blacks, the poor, youth, handicapped, aged and women have mobilized themselves against the establishment and for their respective causes. The number of self-help support and therapy groups addressing every conceivable physical, mental, emotional and social condition has escalated dramatically. Members of these groups often find that the problems do not just lie in their personal ability to accept and cope with the shared condition/problem but with community indifference or negativism and the inadequacies of prevailing professional approaches and institutions. Groups proliferate; action agendas abound; and a new wave of volunteerism is sweeping the country.

To a large degree, the active revolt and subsequent participation in community life of groups heretofore considered "taken care of" is healthy. Identity with a group offers many a sense of dignity, purpose, and power. Everyone is forced to reexamine the limits of "doing for" and "on behalf of" as an approach to achieving human welfare and social justice. The angrier, more adversarial, and more political style of these movements resurrects some strategies for social change which had been out of fashion in periods of growth, optimism, and benevolent cooperation and which needed to be reintroduced. It has clearly demonstrated that meaning well has not been enough and that something different will have to be found to resolve the issues.

On the other hand, the newness of the voices being heard obscures the fact that these participants are volunteers. By this time, thanks to the Lady Bountiful stereotype, to be a volunteer is to be a handmaiden of the establishment. To be a citizen activist is to disassociate oneself from that establishment and its trappings. To be a volunteer means to be white, middle-class, and probably female and thus by definition at least one step removed from the real problems of life. To be a citizen activist is to fight one's own battles in one's own way from the vantage point of really knowing what the fight is all about with no aura of noblesse oblige tainting one's efforts. One result of not recognizing this new wave of activity as volunteer work has been an alienation between what might be called establishment and anti-establishment volunteering.

For the more traditional volunteers, whether or not they are actually white, middle-class or female, it has meant being written off as part of the bumbling, wicked establishment. It has meant having the good intentions they think they possess labeled as phony fronts for a lot of malicious hidden agendas. Many of these volunteers and their organizations are cowering in the corner

56

whimpering: "But we mean well." They wonder if all their efforts have failed, and they are unsure what to do with their individual and collective resources, both financial and human. Others of the more traditional volunteers refuse to acknowledge any validity in the new voices and assume that the timelessness and rightness of their approach will ultimately prevail. It is a tense time for all.

For the anti-establishment volunteers, the alienation starts out feeling more positive. As the newly-activated citizens busily develop their ideas and test their skills, they are often unaware that they are reinventing the wheel. Seeing a need, designing a strategy to address it, establishing an organization to facilitate the process, and recruiting other believers is a pretty exciting and heady experience. However, it is not a new phenomenon, and new wheels can fall into old ruts. Among these ruts are problems of:

---discovering that righteous indignation alone carries a cause only so far

---learning that knowing what one is against does not automatically define what one is for

---obtaining funding and otherwise maintaining an organization or program

---being intolerant of those who ought to see things the way the new group does but do not and

---acting "on their behalf" and "for their own good" anyway.

Wearing blinders, being patronizing, making accommodations to the status quo, and having hidden agendas are not, as it turns out, the exclusive province of the establishment and its volunteer lackeys. The inability of some anti-establishment volunteers and the unwillingness of others to recognize these pitfalls have led or will lead to disillusionment and frustration. Even those whose voluntary action has moved them beyond the pale of volunteer work into anarchy and terrorism understand that the realities of social change require settling in for the long haul. Those interested in

having that change result in a more equitable, democratic society will do well to use all available
resources. These may well include the techniques,
strategies, and energies of the establishment volunteers
as well as the lessons to be learned from their
failures.

Not all anti-establishment volunteering is angry
and political in nature. Some of it is positively
upbeat. Neighborhood youth recreation leagues or
improvement activities, ethnic cultural celebrations,
regional historical events and the like are certainly
happier expressions of citizen concerns than protest
marches. However, they are part of the new wave of
anti-establishment volunteering because they compete,
often successfully, for the attention, affection,
energies and dollars once available to organizations
which are now perceived as establishment but which also
started on an upbeat, apolitical note.

It is not without irony that some of the impetus
for anti-establishment volunteering comes from the
"system" itself. Citizen participation and client
representation have been mandated in many government
social programs, particularly since the 1960's. The
self-development and empowerment of people has been the
thrust of many private religious and secular social
service efforts. The Peace Corps, VISTA, and ACTION
marked an attempt by the Federal government to maximize
the use of government resources in partnership with
volunteer energy and to heighten the visibility and
credibility of the volunteers' role in making society
responsive to the needs of its members.

Some critics have charged that the establishment
jumped on this bandwagon in order to protect itself from
failures and to dump responsibility for social problems
and their solutions on "the people." This is a distinct
possibility which ought not to be ignored by those
seriously interested in resolving specific problems. Whether intentional or unintentional, such
behavior would have an impact on the effectiveness of
everyone's efforts to solve the problems at hand.

Another ramification of the anti-establishment wave
of volunteering which was slower to surface than that

just mentioned is the impact of the mushrooming of single-issue, grassroots and national organizations, each passionately convinced that its mission of direct service and/or advocacy is the top and only priority. The anti-system or, more accurately, systems-changing emphasis which the "downtrodden" have used so successfully at least in making waves has been adopted by a wide range of groups and causes. Some are diametrically opposed to others; all want to win; and few, if any, worry about the consequences of having more and more pieces cut out of a limited pie. While it is not yet clear if and how much the pie is limited, it is certain that blind adherence to a do-as-you-please and let-the-chips-fall-where-they-may attitude on the part of volunteers and organizations will be less viable in the era of the closed frontier. Accountability, priority setting, tradeoffs, coalition building and collaboration have become the new buzz words, and the models for action which would give life to these words are just beginning to be developed. Today's volunteers can choose to view this as a new frontier or to sit back and hope they have picked a winner from among existing establishment and anti-establishment options. A lot is riding on their choices.

4.4 VOLUNTEERS AND THE PECKING ORDER

Another tension in volunteerism which the closing of the frontier has brought to a head is that between volunteers and the staff with whom they work in what has become known as the helping establishment. In the good old days, staff/volunteer relations were not a momentous problem because there were few, if any, staff. As we saw in Chapter 2, it was the activity of volunteers which promoted awareness of certain problems, generated support for the notion that these problems needed to be addressed by the community, and resulted in the creation of new jobs and new professions. In fields where volunteers once reigned supreme, they have been supplanted, often gladly, by paid personnel and have been expected to fill in and around the edges supplementing and supporting the work of staff without interfering with it.

This has involved an almost nonstop changing of assignments and jockeying for position which has left both volunteers and staff wondering if the struggle is worth it. In some areas, the tension manifests itself as a generalized discomfort among both volunteers and staff of not knowing how to live with or without each other. In others, the tension is a very specific concern that the continuing presence of volunteers is a threat to the job security of the paid personnel. In the age of the closed frontier, this is a touchy issue indeed, if real.

Despite serious attempts to clarify and accommodate respective roles, the tensions persist. Their causes have as much to do with the relative position of the helping establishment in the social structure and the relative position of different workers within each field of that establishment as with the attitudes or practices of the individuals involved. There are problems with the pecking order which the involvement of volunteers continuously irritates. They are problems which cannot be solved just by being nice and meaning well.

4.4a "YES, BUT:" THE PUBLIC PERSPECTIVE

The "helping establishment" is not a monolithic entity but rather encompasses that crazy quilt of services and organizations whose creation has already been described. As different philosophies and services have carved a niche for themselves in the scheme of things, communities have invested considerable resources in the helping establishment. However, considerable has not meant unrestricted and has not even necessarily meant enough to assure stability. In other words, the helping establishment is entrenched without being firmly established. Society has said "Yes, the problem should be solved, but do not expect a blank check."

One reason for this tenuous status is the persistent ambivalence among a large segment of society about the nature and causes of various social problems and thus about the appropriateness of corresponding solutions proposed. The very idea that human behavior can be studied scientifically, let alone that that knowledge can be applied to the solution of social problems, is foreign and often downright repugnant to many. Ironically, some of that newfangled data has appeared under the labels of personnel management, new economics, industrial relations, and corporate management and development. In these categories it has been put to work eagerly, since the advancement of industry and commerce is a goal about which society is not ambivalent. It has been a different story when the knowledge is applied, for example, to aiding the economically and emotionally dependent or educating young children.

Even if one accepts the idea of studying and treating human problems scientifically, there are many value judgments to be made. It is one thing to value good health and another to decide whether to care for the sick or provide elaborate public health and preventive medical services. Prisons are needed, but should they be places for punishment or rehabilitation? Mental illness is tragic, but is it safe to house patients in community residences? It is one thing to value a clean environment and another to make tradeoffs necessary to achieve it. Social justice for minorities is easier to support in the abstract than in such specifics as busing or affirmative action. No one should be homeless and hungry, but whose fault is it they are? Children deserve a basic education, but what is basic about art, music, computer and language labs? Libraries, parks, and museums admittedly enrich community life but certainly are dispensable. The list goes on and on.

Another reason for society's "yes, but" perception of the helping establishment is that productivity and success in these social arenas cannot for the most part be measured in terms which make sense to a culture immersed in a bottomline, dollars-and-cents approach to measuring achievement. For example, recidivism rates may provide clues about the effectiveness of services for juvenile delinquents, but how does one know if a juvenile decency or delinquency prevention project has succeeded? How does a professional know that optimum class size or case load is X as opposed to Y? What guarantee is there that more money spent will reduce poverty, make families more stable, assure us that youth with a high school diploma will be able to read and write, etc.?

Furthermore the mechanisms through which the helping establishment operates--not-for-profit corporations or government agencies--seem somehow different from the ultimate American model of successful operation: the for-profit corporation. To be sure, the reasons for and benefits from investing and the relationship of consumer to provider vary between the nonprofit and profit sectors. However, there are many similarities including the structure and function of boards which have not been fully understood and utilized, to the detriment of both.

Aware of its precarious position, the helping establishment has been reluctant to have issues of productivity and accountability closely scrutinized by an already skeptical public, for fear of being misunderstood and of losing what good will and financial support have been gained. There is a tendency to argue that, since the organizations are dealing with complex problems in human lives, we will have to trust their judgment as to whether or not good is being done and being done well. However, the "trust us, we're the experts" defense is getting weaker and more unmarketable in this era of the closed frontier where no cow is too sacred to challenge.

4.4b PROFESSIONALISM: THE INSIDERS' PERSPECTIVE

Actually that defense has always been shaky, for the "expert" status of many practitioners in the helping establishment has never been fully secured. One way to earn the label, particularly in a service area, is to gain recognition as a professional. That was the route chosen by many jobholders in the helping establishment, but some of them got stalled on the road to professional standing. For this discussion, we will refer primarily to social work, teaching, and nursing. They are particularly illustrative of what can happen to would-be professions. However, it should be kept in mind that similar stories can be told about librarians, museum personnel, and various other jobholders in the service institutions.

In everyday parlance, the adjective "professional" is used to distinguish between people who pursue a specific activity for pay and those who do it for free. Or it is a compliment for nearly any jobholder who takes his/her work seriously and does it efficiently and effectively. By this standard, for example, anyone in a given agency from the maintenance man to the executive director can be called professional.

However, the noun profession is used in a somewhat more precise way by insiders or would-be insiders to describe a job/career with the following characteristics:

1. The work is based on a specialized and distinct body of knowledge and has a learned, intellectual character.

2. The knowledge and skills required must be educationally communicable. This usually means extensive academic and practice-oriented training.

3. Practitioners who complete the training are expected to exercise their own judgment and to have autonomy in exercising it. A corollary here is that professional expertise and performance will be appropriately recognized and rewarded.

4. Members of the same profession tend toward self-organization. That is, they form professional associations whose purposes include: to promote standards for admission to the profession, to foster continuing education of practitioners, to monitor accreditation and certification requirements, and to protect the titles by which qualified members are known. All of these are designed not simply to enhance the status of the professionals but to protect the general public as well. An adjunct of characteristics 3 and 4 is that professionals "police" themselves, if necessary.

5. There is a code of ethics and a commitment to a specific objective in a larger social context to which practitioners are expected to adhere.

Social workers, nurses, and teachers are relatively new on the professional scene. As they set out to establish the professional credibility of their disciplines, they tried all the correct motions such as identifying and developing a knowledge base, increasing standards for entrance to the profession, certifying training institutions, establishing professional organizations and protecting titles. From their beginnings they have been recognized as having the appropriate professional dedication and ethical commitment. Yet on nearly every other criterion of "profession" they have been relatively unsuccessful in convincing other disciplines and the larger community that theirs are "real" professions. What has happened?

To begin with, the knowledge base of these new professions is not always perceived as valid. Social work and teaching are built on social and behavioral sciences which are themselves new kids on the academic block. Sociology and psychology lack the glamour and mystique of physical sciences, mathematics, and technology. They do not have the long tradition and respectability of the humanities. They have had their own status and credibility problems as legitimate academic disciplines within the ivory tower. One defense used by "pure" social scientists has been to become more academic, more intellectual, more "objective" and more abstract. An outgrowth of this is sometimes feeling superior to those in applied fields, even when what is being applied is the social scientific knowledge being generated by the academicians. At first glance, nurses might be viewed as having the advantage of a more secure or at least more respectable knowledge base. However, they have found that the professional recognition surrounding the practice of medicine has largely been awarded to doctors and the nurses' membership on the medical team perceived as having a water boy function.

Closely related to skepticism about their knowledge bases is the idea that social workers, nurses, and teachers are doing work which just about anyone could do if they had to or wanted to. Differences between listening to a neighbor's problems over coffee and casework counseling, between teaching one's children and a few friends how to tie knots and presenting a complete curriculum to a class of thirty, or between tending a sick relative and supervising a cardiac care unit are not appreciated. And surely these skills cannot compare to that of a psychiatrist, a university professor, or a cardiologist. Or can they?

In addition, these are not, for the most part, professions which are practiced autonomously. Practitioners generally operate as components of larger organizations and by design are supervised by more experienced practitioners or administrators. This has cost them some of the aura of authority and expertise traditionally granted to "real" professionals as well as meaning that they have to deal with problems of bureaucracy, organization maintenance and the like. It is ironic that this has been held against the new professions now that we are beginning to appreciate that professional autonomy sometimes becomes professional arrogance and professional expertise becomes a shield for protected incompetence. The abuses of professional status in the "real" professions have led to a re-examination of accountability which may ultimately benefit the status of newer fields and, more importantly, the well-being of clients.

The refinement of job descriptions and work assignments which has resulted in the introduction of paraprofessionals, technicians, aides and assorted other "nonprofessionals" ought to have enhanced the professional status of trained social workers, nurses, and teachers. However, it does not seem to have paid off in that regard. It merely seems to have increased the cost of doing work which society is not sure it wants done and has complicated problems of pecking order among the insiders.

What this all adds up to is that these professions have never been recognized and recompensed at the same level as doctors, lawyers, engineers, business executives, etc. The administrative positions in each field have been rewarded somewhat more adequately, probably because they represent the business end of the operation. Social work, nursing and teaching quickly became women's professions and have remained so in image and fact, though men have found niches in administration out of proportion to their numbers in the professions. When society's ambivalence about caring in general and the competition for status in each field are added to the issues surrounding the status of women, you have the

65

makings of the vicious cycle which has plagued these three professions. As it stands now, Lady Bountiful with a paycheck has many of the same problems as Lady Bountiful unpaid. The stern discipline of the old maid school teacher has more charm than psychology-based motivational techniques of today's educator. The "lady with the lamp" who tended to every sickbed need of her patients is more palatable than today's monitor of life-support machines.

Because the professionalization strategy appears to be a dead-end street, some practitioners have tried unionization as a means for gaining sufficient clout to improve their positions in the workplace. However, in doing so, they have risked and, in many ways, lost the one chunk of professional status which they had gained: appreciation of their dedication and commitment to their respective causes. Always uncertain what to do with selfless dedication on anybody's part, the general public is relieved to hear demands expressed in terms already understood such as better pay and working conditions. To understand what these might have to do with improving services involves subtleties with which most people are reluctant to deal for reasons already discussed. It is easier to deal with the money issues. This selective hearing by the public and the aforementioned selective telling by the "experts" leave large gaps in everyone's ability to deal with the basic issues. It remains to be seen whether unionization will be any more effective a tool than professionalization in achieving adequate recognition for paid personnel in helping fields, greater effectiveness in providing services, or both.

4.4c CAUGHT IN THE SQUEEZE

It is not too early, however, to see that all of this activity fosters the image of volunteers as well-intentioned but amateurish dabblers and pushes them lower in the pecking order. This affects different volunteers in different ways.

Least affected at this point are the new anti-establishment or extra-establishment volunteers described above. Caught up in the zeal of their new crusades, they are often either "unburdened" by the presence of paid staff or are just beginning to build organizations of sufficient complexity to warrant the hiring of staff. As they move in this direction, they would do well to remember that staff/volunteer tension is another rut into which the reinvented wheel may fall as innocently as the original model.

Almost as oblivious to the impact of pecking order problems on the status of volunteers are the policy development volunteers, particularly those on boards of directors in helping establishment agencies. Board members tend to perceive themselves and are often perceived as doing their civic duty rather than doing volunteer work. They have not felt too obliged to worry about the degree to which they are performing effectively. For the most part, they have been the group which has accepted the "trust us, we're the experts" stance of staff. They have assumed that giving virtually free rein to staff is the appropriately respectful approach and have often abdicated their own legal and ethical responsibility as corporate managers and trustees. The tensions of the closed frontier are forcing boards to assess their own performance and to make them more aware of the very complex issues of staff/volunteer relationships and labor/management conflict.

Pecking order problems have had their most immediate impact on those volunteers who are involved in the everyday operations of an organization. The fill-in-the-cracks approach to volunteering subscribed to by both volunteers and staff often leads to the volunteers being asked to do odds and ends. If these tasks are not clearly defined and mutually understood and appreciated, they create a nuisance for staff and a frustrating, possibly even demeaning experience for volunteers.

At a more basic level, the presence of volunteers, however satisfying individual assignments and relationships may be, is a threat to paid personnel in the precariously perched helping establishment. Old bromides such as "volunteers supplement not supplant staff" or "volunteers are important members of the service team" do not by themselves ease the discomfort. These catchy phrases lack precision and sensitivity in recognizing the wide range of skills included in the word "staff" and the wide range of skills volunteers bring. The concern about job security may well be valid, depending on the particular paid position and whether or not it is perceived as one where we could "make do" with volunteers if the chips go down. For starters, consider the following. The national executive director of a youth-serving agency is not threatened in the same way as the recreation worker in a local branch. The local executive is less threatened than the receptionist. A neurosurgeon can feel more secure than a nurse's aide. All could conceivably lose if the helping establishment collapses. However, it seems more likely that changes would be by erosion than explosion, a situation which encourages suspicion of volunteer involvement.

From the other vantage point, volunteers are confronted not only with assaults on their self-image but also with some tough ethical decisions about where they belong. In the extreme case of a school or hospital strike, for example, what side should the volunteer be on? What action is appropriate? Every option is unacceptable to someone. Should volunteers break picket lines in order to keep minimum services in operation out of concern for the welfare of current patients or students? Should they instead stay neutral with the hope that a settlement will produce long-term gains which outweigh short-term disruptions? Should they perceive themselves as one of the parties involved and demand a voice in the settlement? If so, are they demanding a voice as volunteers per se or as clients, advocates, taxpayers, parents, or some combination of all these? The absolute right and wrong which different factions see so clearly in the heat of the moment do not shed much light for the serious volunteer.

While the example of strikes may seem a bit remote from routine issues surrounding staff/volunteer relations, it is really only a particularly dramatic expression of those thorny questions. That strikes are even a possibility in these areas says much about our times. How we learn to cope with them and the deeper issues they represent will affect many aspects of national life, including the role of volunteering.

4.5 PROFESSIONALIZING THE VOLUNTEER

In a move which brings to mind the maxim that the more things change the more they stay the same, another significant trend in volunteerism is the revolt of volunteers and their supporters among paid personnel. Frustrated with their position in society, some volunteers have not exercised their option of abandoning volunteer work altogether. Rather they have sought to improve their status by demanding proper recognition and support for their efforts. Most are advocating professionalism for volunteers, though occasional voices are heard suggesting unions and guilds.

Like their models in the paid professions, volunteer advocates argue with considerable validity that volunteers are essential resources in modern society. Better trained, more respected, more "professional" volunteers will be happier in their assignments and more effective in their jobs. Furthermore volunteers should be encouraged to approach the selection of volunteer work in the same way they would evaluate career alternatives, so that their needs and aspirations are understood and hence put to better use for everyone's benefit.

In addition, society should give more recognition to the value of volunteer work by making sure that tax benefits are given to all volunteers whether they itemize deductions or not, that the expenses of volunteer work are built into budgets, that volunteer time is "priced" and used as in-kind credit for fundraising purposes, and that volunteer work is treated as work experience for the volunteer's overall career development.

Creating a professionalized niche for volunteers will require a reassessment of individual attitudes and general public opinion. It will necessitate a realignment of organizational structures and methods of operation. That the process is underway is evident in the literature, in the rise of new mechanisms such as Voluntary Action Centers, in the creation of new paid positions such as Volunteer Co-ordinator, and in legislative activity on issues like those listed above. The "professional volunteer" may well be an idea whose time has come. Its implementation might just help strengthen the relative position of the entire helping establishment. Its ultimate success, however, may hinge on the degree to which its supporters understand the pitfalls as well as the possibilities inherent in professionalization.

4.6 SOME CLOSING THOUGHTS

There are other changes occurring in the workplace which have a bearing on the future of volunteering, though which direction they will lead is yet to be determined. For the most part they reflect the growing demand of the general public to have all facets of life viewed as important, not just that portion of it in which one's livelihood is earned. There are indications that more people will have more leisure time. Experiments are underway with alternative work patterns such as flextime and shared positions. Some corporations are trying out released-time and social service leaves for those employees who have an interest in community service projects. Early retirement may mean a longer period for relaxation or for new adventures among those senior citizens whose physical and financial position permit it. There is much talk that these changes are coming or are here. Many are not really widespread enough to be called trends, and the economic realities of the 80's may interrupt or eliminate some. However, even if they do take hold, it does not automatically follow that more people will choose to volunteer. It does at least suggest new recruitment sources, new audiences to which to appeal.

Even the trend which has been bemoaned as a threat to volunteerism may prove beneficial in the long run: the influx of women into the workplace. As more women have chosen careers or been forced to seek employment, their availability and willingness to volunteer have decreased. Lady Bountiful's disappearance from the volunteer scene where she had been taken for granted so long had people believing for a while that volunteerism was practically dead. As the shock of this change has worn off, it has added impetus to the reassessment of volunteering and the readjustment of ways of working which, as we have seen, is underway for many reasons.

To sum up this exploration of the status of volunteering and how it came about, a homely analogy may help. Volunteerism has rightly been viewed as an integral part of the fabric of American society. Its texture and colors have changed over the years. It was never sewn with a particular pattern in mind; and it is definitely old and badly wrinkled.

Some believe it is so worn and ragged that it should be thrown out or at least packed carefully away with other cultural heirlooms like calling cards. Others, including this writer, believe that this particular brand of homespun is sturdier than that and can survive more than a gentle brushing or sloppy patching. It needs a good airing, which has been the purpose of the chapters so far, and a good pressing, which will be the focus of subsequent ones.

RESOURCES

Adams, Margaret. "The Compassion Trap" in WOMAN IN SEXIST SOCIETY: STUDIES IN POWER AND POWERLESS- NESS. Edited by Vivian Gornick and Barbara K. Moran. New York: Basic Books, Inc., 1971.

Bakal, Carl. CHARITY USA. New York: Times Books, 1979.

Etzioni, Amitai, ed. THE SEMI-PROFESSIONS AND THEIR ORGANIZATION: TEACHERS, NURSES, SOCIAL WORKERS. New York: Free Press, 1969.

Joslyn, Kerstin. "A Nation of Volunteers: Participa- tory Democracy or Administrative Manipula- tion?" BERKELEY JOURNAL OF SOCIOLOGY (1973-74), pp. 159-181.

Katz, Harvey. GIVE! WHO GIVES YOUR CHARITY DOL- LAR? Garden City, NY: Anchor Press/Doubleday, 1974.

McCurley, Stephen. "Volunteer-Union Relations: Thoughts and Warnings." VOLUNTARY ACTION LEADERSHIP, Summer, 1979, pp. 15-16.

Nisbet, Robert A. TWILIGHT OF AUTHORITY. New York: Oxford University Press, 1975.

SECTION II

EFFECTIVE VOLUNTEERS:

PERSPECTIVES ON THE PRESENT

5

A BASIC FRAMEWORK

5.1 TAKING DILEMMAS BY THE HORN

One purpose for the walk we have just taken through American social history thinking "volunteer" was to refresh our memories about the pervasiveness of the phenomenon. As we knew or suspected, one would be hard pressed to find a facet of American life which has not at some point felt the impact of volunteerism. It is one of the mechanisms which American society has provided more by default than design for those among its citizens who want to play an active role in shaping the ways in which society meets the needs of its individual members by doing more than just looking out for themselves and giving more than lip service to social concerns.

A more important purpose of the historical review than enumerating the organizations, institutions, and trends which volunteerism has influenced was the development of a better understanding of the forces which have shaped volunteerism. What we have seen is a phenomenon which seemed to spring naturally from the energies and ideals of pioneering individuals who found themselves working together in increasingly complex situations to forge a new, free, growing society. Volunteering blossomed willy-nilly in many settings and in many forms. It has become so much a part of the social landscape that it is hardly given a second glance.

By our definition of volunteering, we are talking about activities which fall under the general heading of doing good and which are therefore open to a wide range of value-laden interpretations and perceptions. There has been a tendency among those who do give it a second glance to assume that the effect of volunteer efforts has been positive, or at least not negative, for society at large. After all, if one faction of volunteers gets too carried away on a given issue, rest assured that there will be another group fighting that fire with a volunteer fire of its own. If still other volunteers are dabbling in activity which seems inconsequential or extraneous at the moment, what is the harm in letting them keep busy that way? In either case, there is no point in making a mountain out of a molehill by paying too much attention to the whole thing.

Ironically one result of taking volunteering for granted and viewing it as a means of "doing what comes naturally" has been to make a molehill out of a mountain. By not paying enough attention to the mechanism itself, our images of what it is and how it operates have been allowed to degenerate into belittling stereotypes which conflict with what is known about the nature and scope of volunteering today. It has been assumed that the rationales and motivations for volunteering are so fragile that we have to treat both the subject and the practitioners very gingerly. Again this contradicts evidence of the phenomenon's resilience. Finally it has been assumed that we have to wait for other social forces to shape our perceptions and definitions of volunteer work.

While this analysis is interesting in itself, the main purpose of Section I was to provide a foundation for discussing what we can do to shape volunteerism to meet the present and projected needs of society. It is clear from our review of America's two hundred years of experience with volunteerism that the mechanism has so far survived disinterest, ambivalence, contradictions and tensions. It promises, or threatens if that is your point of view, to remain a significant force in society. The issue now seems to be not whether volunteerism will continue but whether it can be maintained in forms which in fact contribute to the common good.

Another lesson to be learned from volunteer history is that volunteers have made their substantive contributions because they believed in articulating their perceptions of problems and solutions and then acting on these definitions. This approach has been applied to volunteerism by its critics. In many areas we have them to thank for our insights into some of its limitations. It is time that the same approach be applied to volunteering by those of us who believe that volunteers are a national resource, a form of social capital, if you will. We have tried the pat-on-the-head approach and found it to be more a way to damn with faint praise. We have tried working with volunteerism as it has been defined by other forces and have found that to be an insidious form of shadow boxing. The time has come to take a stand on the various important issues which volunteering as a mechanism has raised and then to develop practices based on those stands.

Taking firm stands is not equivalent to issuing a decree in the ongoing debate about whether volunteering is priceless or worthless. Its purpose is to enable us to cull from our knowledge and experience those pieces of volunteerism which are relevant and useful today and to ensure that they are given the opportunity to be used to full advantage. The remainder of this chapter then will spell out those general positions which this writer believes to be most useful. They will serve as the basic framework for the rest of the book in which we will apply these positions to our dealings as or with volunteers.

5.2 RESPONSIBILITIES AND RIGHTS

Curiously the right to volunteer is the most basic and most universally accessible privilege of American citizenship, more basic and available than even the right to vote. As a unique expression of individual freedom and free enterprise at work on social concerns, it has been allowed to flourish relatively unbridled by the checks-and-balances approach which has been gradually built into other facets of community life and especially in government and business. To be sure, there have been some constraints of law placed on voluntary organizations and some of the volunteers within them. These will be discussed in greater detail in later chapters. What is at issue here is a less tangible, attitudinal problem whereby, for a variety of historical reasons, it has been all too easy for volunteers to say in practice, if not in words, "I have the right to do whatever I wish whenever I wish to do it as it pertains to doing good. Because I mean well and am willing to do this for free solely out of the goodness of my heart, I should not be challenged or thwarted in any way." Furthermore, it has been all too easy for the rest of us to say, "Fine. Go to it."

The right to volunteer exists de facto and is to be cherished as fervently as any other right of citizenship. However, by definition, volunteering is not a private act engaged in by consenting adults. It is by definition a public effort, whether publicized or not, to shape the way in which society treats its members. As such, society has the right to curtail excesses and abuses, by law if that becomes necessary. More importantly, society has the right to expect that those who choose to exercise the option of volunteering and those who encourage and foster it do so responsibly.

Unfortunately, degree of responsibility is not an absolute concept. However, we can look at certain experiences and be a little more forthright in acknowledging that privileges carry responsibilities in volunteering as in everything else. For example, it is not responsible to agree to be a big brother or sister to a troubled youth, one of whose identified needs is for a positive and reliable adult friend, IF you intend only to visit with that child when you have nothing else to do or when it makes you feel good. It is not responsible to recruit baseball coaches or Scout leaders IF you know their primary interest will be in meeting their own ego needs even when that conflicts with the developmental needs of the children involved. It is not proper to agree to membership on a board of directors IF you intend only to lend your name to the letterhead and do not expect to make the meetings. It is irresponsible to assume that your willingness to do good for free automatically qualifies you for a volunteer task without any additional training. It is irresponsible to establish a new voluntary organization on the pretext that it is doing good, thereby demanding tax-exempt status and community support, IF the only real reason for its existence is to give its founder a new pond in which to be a big fish.

The "ifs" in the above illustrations were emphasized on purpose to show that, while these are factors which legitimately and often constructively come into play in the complex business of volunteerism, they should not be used as excuses for denying that volunteers have a responsibility to the larger society. To be a responsible volunteer is not to act on the basis of absolute definitions of what constitutes doing good and out of totally selfless motivation. It is rather to act as intentionally, sincerely, and knowledgeably as possible and to be aware that accountability does and should exist. Many will find this notion foreign; for some it will be unpalatable. These reactions can be dealt with positively. Those who find it unacceptable should exercise their option not to get involved with volunteering.

5.3 VOLUNTEERING AS WORK NOT PLAY

Despite the fact that the realities of what constitutes work have been undergoing almost constant change since the good old twenty-five hour days of the frontier, we still tend to view real work as those activities by which we earn a livelihood and otherwise ensure survival. Since, for most people, earning a living means being paid in cash, we associate real work with those activities whose value is measured in dollars. Everything else is play or, to be a bit classier, a leisure time activity.

Volunteering aside for a moment, the work/play dichotomy is not as clear as we pretend. Some people's ideas of play strike others as odd forms of relaxation. For example, to the nonrunner, neither jogging around the neighborhood nor running a marathon qualifies as fun. Tournament bridge and league bowling require a serious commitment and a substantial degree of organization which many employers would welcome among their employees on the job. Even the workplace is not "all work and no play." Some people actually enjoy their jobs. Regardless of that, coffee breaks, lunch hours, and company-sanctioned or informal recreation programs are examples of opportunities which provide companionship and a change of pace acknowledged as important to workers' well-being and productivity.

The important distinction between work and play, for our purposes at any rate, is that the latter exists to entertain and refresh the participant. Thus, by definition, volunteering does not qualify as play. However, semantic precision is not really our concern. A far more serious consequence of treating volunteering as play solely because it is not real paid work has been the tendency of some groups who depend on volunteers to spend so much time keeping the volunteers happy doing their own thing that the group's primary purpose is pushed aside. Some volunteers, hiding behind their presumed rights, have compounded this by expecting recreation and by leaving the minute the activity is no longer fun and games. Yet nearly everyone is reluctant to reject the so-called services of the recreation-minded volunteer even when shown to be more interference than help in promoting the cause at hand.

Without discounting the common-sense wisdom of making volunteering pleasurable and companionable, it is much more useful to view it as work than as play. For one thing this implies a different kind of social purpose which should encourage both the volunteer and the users of volunteer services to take the activities more seriously. Furthermore the concept of work suggests that those tasks can be grouped into units called jobs and can be treated as such.

For the "employer" this would mean giving some thought to defining the jobs to be done, developing job descriptions and jobholder qualifications, and enumerating job requirements like hours, supplies and workspace. It suggests that careful attention be paid to recruitment, screening, training, and supervision of the jobholder. Yes, it even dares to include the option of turning down an applicant or firing a recruit who has not worked out on the job. However, this should not be construed as license to be any more arbitrary or cavalier about dismissing a volunteer than present laws and personnel practices allow in relation to paid employees.

A much-overlooked fact is that volunteers are not "free help." Where the time of paid staff is used in working with volunteers and where specific expenses can be anticipated in relation to supplies, training, recognition events, and the like, the dollar and time costs can be estimated. Even where the "employer" is another volunteer, there is a price of time and energy to be paid in working with other volunteers, and this ought to be evaluated. In all cases, the costs should be projected and budgeted. Interestingly, the investment is usually worth it, and the often-heard sentiment that "it's easier to do it myself" is frequently a cover-up for poor planning and poor management.

Using the work model to look at the "employee's" point of view, we can further assert that volunteers do not work for free. They expect all the same payments and paybacks for their services that a "real" employee does except salaries and wages. These expectations can include: doing something useful; helping others; using present skills; developing new ones; finding companionship; earning appreciation, recognition and, where appropriate, advancement. All of these are reasonable and can be mutually beneficial. Other motivations are a little more troublesome but not necessarily negative. The volunteer who thinks he owes a friend a favor or the one who feels guilty about saying no may be harder to inspire. However, there are some jobs for which these are sufficient. The key is to have a recruitment and selection process which deals with why the volunteer wishes to be involved and then uses that information for proper placement.

Of course, there are some areas where the work/job concept as it relates to volunteering varies somewhat from paid-in-cash work. In volunteer work the "employer" has less control over determining how many hours the volunteer will work. This is as it should be. While volunteering is work, it is a kind of moonlighting. Volunteers have other responsibilities, family- and business-related, to which they are entitled to give priority. A sick child is just as valid an excuse for absence from volunteer work as a hastily scheduled business meeting. The appropriate response is to treat these factors with as much flexibility and sensitivity as possible when defining volunteer job requirements without abdicating the right to say, "It appears that our needs and your availability do not mesh."

Also with volunteer work, recruitment is often a dignified way of saying begging. Even if we had personnel offices--and in communities with Voluntary Action Centers we sort of do, the waiting rooms are not likely to be overflowing with eager applicants. Nonetheless, there is little to be gained by either employer or employee from the come-whenever-you-can-and-do-whatever-you-wish-because we-really-need-your-help appeal on which many organizations rely.

Any resemblance in this section to sound personnel management is not coincidental. In theory it seems too obvious an approach to require mention. Practice, however, has been a different story. More specific applications of the work/job concept will be discussed in the next two chapters.

5.4   THE LONE RANGER RIDES NO MORE

Among the most appealing components in our present images of volunteers are those of people helping people in heartwarming one-to-one situations or pitching in on an upbeat neighborhood self-help project. In some of the pictures thus conjured up, there are only two people, the gratified helper and the grateful helped, against a backdrop of nothing except possibly a hanging plant. In other mental or real pictures, we see a determined and happy group of folks who have just pulled themselves up by their own bootstraps. The purpose of these images is to show that volunteers are the people who really care what happens to their fellow human beings and/or are willing to help each other out, the system be hanged. These images make wonderful media blurbs and provide fodder for after-dinner speeches. They strike a nerve in all of us which has been jarred by the insensitivity, incompetence, imper-sonality and imperviousness of many organizations and institutions in our society.

We envision ourselves singlehandedly charging into a given situation and stamping out the evil at hand in much the same way the Lone Ranger pulled off his feats. We more often settle for sharing such victories vicariously and touting them as the way things ought to be, with good folks triumphing over the evil establish-ment. Perhaps these images also serve as a defense mechanism for volunteers who are struggling to maintain self-respect in a society which has succeeded in pushing them lower and lower in the pecking order of recogni-tion.

Comforting as these thoughts may be, they are a delusion. Have we forgotten that even the Lone Ranger often worked with the sheriff? Do we know how he subsisted? Was it by in-kind grants of goods and services from Tonto's tribe? What happened to law and order in communities which did not have a Lone Ranger? Did it screech to a halt? As farfetched as this analogy may be, it is no more ridiculous than pretending that volunteers work totally independently and are at their best when they ignore or are immune to the system. Did we notice that the volunteer in our picture was put in touch with the needy under the auspices of an agency? Did we realize that the neighborhood project was funded by a foundation grant?

The System does not exist. We live and work in numerous interrelated social systems, some of which are more complex, pervasive, and powerful than others, to be sure. However, all are fluid, vulnerable to attack at some points, and susceptible to change. The point of equilibrium, i.e., the so-called status quo, is constantly shifting, however slight the movement may seem in any given period of time. It is more productive to look at which systems volunteers operate in than to pretend they exist apart.

To saddle volunteerism with a nonsystems orientation is to deny volunteers the opportunity to deal with the realities of community service and social change in modern society. For one thing it encourages a lot of simplistic thinking about returning to the good old days of individual self-reliance, general neighborliness, and the presumed absence of outside parties interfering in basic human relationships. For example, in times past when the most effective treatment for many illnesses was holding the hands of the dying, we did not need hospitals with expensive staff and equipment. If, with the miraculous advances in medical science, we have gone to the other extreme and forgotten that there comes a time when the best service still available is to hold the hands of the dying, it does not have to follow that we should dismantle the medical establishment. It can also suggest a wide range of opportunities to improve it, some dramatic and some not.

A more immediate and equally insidious ramification of the nonsystems orientation is that it grants a monopoly on meaning well to volunteers and not all volunteers at that, just those who work in one-to-one or grass-roots settings preferably on their own. This leads to overglorifying some individual acts which, if we are honest, are best described as self-serving, self-righteous, or even arrogant. There is a moral in the old joke about the eager beaver Boy Scout who whisks an old lady across the street and is totally oblivious to her protests that she does not want to cross. The monopoly also creates a hierarchy among volunteers in which the Lone Ranger types are deemed to mean "better" and to care more about people than those who serve on boards and committees. This conflicts with another perceived hierarchy of volunteers which defines boards and committee work as the top of the ladder in terms of the class and sophistication required. The social action volunteers, of course, have their own perceptions of how best to mean well. Furthermore, it must come as a shock and an affront to social service staff to learn that by accepting a paycheck and working within an organized setting they have forfeited the option of doing any good.

The interpersonal tensions which this monopoly engenders might be amusing if they were not so counterproductive. Modern psychology has given us many important insights into motivation, the concept of hidden agenda being one. We know now that even the Lone Ranger had highly selfish as well as abstractly noble purposes. Noblesse oblige may not be the total engima we once thought. This can be very helpful. Certainly it is refreshing and useful to be able to acknowledge that in helping others we do not need to be ashamed to allow as how this meets some of our own needs. However, when application of these insights turns into an argument over who is more noble than whom or, conversely, whose motives are more sullied than whose, what we have is a diversionary tactic. When it results in time and energy being spent in search of absolute purity and absolute good as if these were either prerequisites for action or excuses for inappropriate and harmful behavior, what we have is time and energy wasted.

The nobility and purity trap in which it is easy to become ensnared on a personal and interpersonal level has the same pitfalls in a broader systems approach to doing good. If we assume that real do-gooding can only take place around causes and in organizations whose stated purpose is to help people, we may miss some opportunities to make all the systems in our society more responsive and more acountable for their successes or failures as measured in progress toward human welfare, human dignity, and social justice. For example, it is quite possible for a social service organization aided by its volunteer and staff personnel to be so preoccupied with its own survival that it in fact does very little good. It is equally possible that somewhere on the hidden agenda of a big corporation whose stated purpose and top priority is to make a profit is the genuine recognition of responsibility to contribute to the common good in other ways like arranging for employees to do volunteer work on company time. Even if it can be "proved" beyond the shadow of a doubt that the corporation's "real" reason for encouraging this activity is because it increases employee morale and productivity, is that a crime? Perhaps it is, if those employees are released to do busy work for the social service organization mentioned above and all parties involved assume they have thereby fulfilled their civic duty once and for all.

Although a systems orientation raises extremely complex and perhaps unresolvable issues, it does offer some possibilities for refining our perceptions of volunteer work and the practices based on those perceptions, possibilities which are obscured by a simplistic heroes-and-villains approach. Reluctant as we may be to let go of romantic myths about white-hat volunteers, we will find it more useful to acknowledge that the Lone Ranger probably never did ride alone but in any event rides alone no more.

5.5   CHAINS OF ACCOUNTABILITY

No one is more painfully aware than the writer that the basic framework which has thus far been proposed presents as many questions as it answers. It is one thing to take the dilemmas by the horns philosophically and to assert that volunteers have responsibilities as well as rights, that volunteering is work not play, and that volunteering is not best viewed merely as an individual act of goodness. It is quite another to make these assertions any more useful than the myths and ambivalences they were intended to counteract. Carried to overzealous, illogical extremes, any one of them might produce behavior as bizarre as anything we have seen yet. If there is any way out of these messes--the one we started with and the one created by this framework, it is probably the way we got into them: one step at a time. The following are proposed:

Step 1. Accept the principle of accountability.

A common element in the different facets of the proposed framework is the idea that volunteering is not conducted in a vacuum. By viewing it as an individual pastime extraneous to real life or real work we have based our behavior on assumptions which have unnecessarily constrained the role of volunteers. These constraints have reduced, if not precluded, volunteers' effectiveness in doing what they think they are doing which is making a positive contribution, be it small or grandiose, to promoting a more humane society. The purpose of suggesting that our individual and collective approach to volunteering include some notion of accountability is not to repress the passion, commitment, and freedom of individual volunteers or, tempting though it is, to control the outcome of their efforts. Rather it is to give volunteerism sufficient structure and support to remain a viable mechanism in a society which purports to care about the welfare of its members.

Furthermore, accountability is not a one-way street at the end of which we will hear society say "jump" and the volunteers reply "how high"? Accountability implies building mutual respect and obligation among all parties involved in order to make the best use of all resources available for meeting the challenges at hand. All of this becomes particularly relevant and urgent in an era of closed-in frontiers where we are grappling with the finiteness of resources.

As if accountability were not a ponderous enough concept by itself, the heading of this section, Chains of Accountability, threatens to make us feel even more weighed down. It does not need to have a shackling effect. This particular choice of words is intended only to take advantage of the immediate visual image which chains bring to mind: interlocking, interdependent links which need to be equally strong if they are to work. The image of a chain suggests more of the complexities and dynamics inherent in society and thus volunteerism today than the customary line on a typical organization chart. If the image haunts us a little with fears that we are either putting all this effort into making a paper chain or into making one that is too heavy to be useful, that will not be all bad because it means we are thinking. However, our major concentration will be on strengthening the links which affect volunteerism. If we do not get swept away with the semantic bliss which the metaphor engenders, it just may be useful.

Step 2.   Strengthen existing chains of accountability.

Accountability is not all that revolutionary an idea in relation to volunteering. Much volunteer work takes place in organized group settings which include but are not restricted to the formal, incorporated social service agency. Where two or three are gathered together to organize for a stated purpose, account-ability is implicit, at least within the group. As the organization grows, so does the division of labor and the need for greater clarity about who is accountable for what. While we have fostered the former, we have not been as successful with the latter. Thus our focus in the rest of Section II will be on opportunities and pitfalls for improving accountability in existing volunteer structures.

To do this we will group the common types of volunteer tasks under two headings which describe the major functions for which those structures are already accountable regardless of the subject matter with which they work:

Policy-making Chain--volunteers who work in groups
(Chapter 6)   within an organization such as committees, boards, and task forces. The purpose of the groups is to produce policies, program goals, and general procedures which enable the organization to fulfill its mission.

Operations Chain --   volunteers who work in direct
(Chapter 7)   service to clients, assist in organization maintenance, engage in advocacy/social action, or in any way help implement the program and policy goals established in the policy chain.

Note: Although social action volunteers sometimes view themselves as a breed apart, those who do their advocacy thing in an organization context are in practice accountable for policy and operations in the same ways as other volunteers.

In keeping with the assertion that accountability is a two-way street, Chapter 8 will be devoted to a discussion of those ways in which society can improve on its already formalized treatment of volunteers. We will look at issues which deserve the attention of those whose subject matter as well as whose mechanism is volunteerism.

Step 3. Expand the concept of accountability to apply to other forms of volunteering, some existing and some to be created.

If we can improve present practices and understandings of accountability, we will have accomplished no small task. However, we will only have won a few battles and not the larger war, that being the continued development of society's effectiveness in addressing human issues and social problems. Because in a democratic and pluralistic society there is no one eternal set of values and beliefs which will settle the issues once and for all, we need to create opportunities, processes, and mechanisms for citizens to use in this ongoing effort. Thus in Section III we will look again at the full spectrum of voluntary activity which may fairly be called volunteer work, show how each may contribute, and see what new techniques and new types of volunteering may be needed in the future.

6

POLICY VOLUNTEERING

6.1 ELEMENTARY, MY DEAR VOLUNTEER

The transformation of a social concern into a formal social cause via a series of organizational steps is quite logical. The fact that this transformation has occurred repeatedly suggests that it makes a good deal of sense and must have something going for it. At this point, much volunteering takes place in established organizations where volunteers are recruited to fill already more or less designed niches in a larger structure without having to give much thought to how that structure came to be. Even those whose perception of meeting certain needs leads them to establish still another organization often follow the developmental patterns of existing ones without fully understanding why. Logical or not, these practices are not automatically useful and, like everything else we have looked at so far, cannot be taken for granted.

Picking up where we left off in the previous chapter, the scenario goes something like this: A person or handful of people decides that a specific concern is a problem they wish to tackle. They round up a few like-minded individuals and begin meeting to discuss their concerns and what they feel can be done about them. It is not long before some tasks are defined and assignments made, often one designating a leader. Everyone pitches in to do what must be done, and the decision making is done together in a style reminiscent of the New England town meeting.

If the perceived problem has any complexity at all, as it usually does, the need for an ongoing mechanism, i.e., an organization, soon becomes evident. Before you know it, temporary officers have been elected and a committee formed to draft some formal statement about the group's purpose and structure. Usually this produces a set of bylaws. A fundraising committee has probably been put into motion, and the member with the best typewriter corralled into doing the necessary clerical work. Everyone else assures support for the activities and work being generated. A board of directors is soon created. Most organizations find it advantageous to incorporate under the appropriate laws pertaining to the not-for-profit corporation. The advantage of this move is not just an intangible addition to the group's credibility; it also carries with it some very tangible ramifications for funding. For example, if a group can demonstrate that it is a charitable, religious, educational or similar community service organization, it may be granted tax-exempt status and thus become eligible to solicit and receive funds from foundations, government agencies, United Ways, or donors who appreciate the tax benefits.

Another way community groups get started is when the original core of concerned individuals has not simply identified a problem but has also decided that the way to solve it is to follow an organization pattern already established elsewhere. Often this will be a model offered by a state or national organization. In this case, the organizers are not starting from scratch in designing the response. While these groups go through many start-up motions similar to those already outlined, they are likely also to be directing their activities toward meeting the requirements for affiliation with or accreditation by the parent organization.

This start-up process does not happen without much commitment, involvement, enthusiasm and sacrifice among the individual members. Yet almost unobtrusively, three very important things are happening to the organization which will have a profound effect on the relations of individual participants within the cause. First, a DIVISION OF LABOR has been created--and for very good reasons. Most obviously, there is more work to be done than any one individual can do. More hands can make the work load manageable for each person and can make it possible for the organization to accomplish its work in a more effective and timely manner. Even if one or two people are willing and able to do all of the specific tasks at hand, they will find that others whose support is needed want to "do something useful." This usually means more than giving adulation to the initiators. Hence it becomes politically as well as practically important to share the work and increase the number of people who have a clear stake in its outcome.

Furthermore, a division of labor allows for recognition that different pieces of work may require different skills and will be more effectively accomplished if assigned to persons with appropriate skills or at least with an interest in and potential for developing them. When the time and expertise required to conduct some facets of the work exceeds that available among the volunteers, staff may be hired, and the resulting division of labor becomes quite specialized.

A second factor which slipped into the situation with the designation of temporary leadership is FORMALIZED ACCOUNTABILITY. In the most rudimentary stages, formal accountability will be almost exclusively internal and may, in fact, not seem too formal at all. It will feel more like an agreement among friends to do certain tasks and get back to each other. As assignments proliferate and mechanisms such as boards and committees are created, accountability is defined more systematically. Once a group decides to incorporate, to affiliate with a larger body, and/or to accept funds from outside sources, its formal accountability extends beyond its own membership and constituency in very precise legal and contractual terms. For example, when staff is hired, a board becomes responsible for complying with laws governing employment practices. Compliance with local, state and federal laws applies to any property and facilities owned by the corporation and may be germane to various programs, services and activities of the organization.

Finally, a corporate entity with its own existence has been established. This CORPORATENESS is structured and should not be confused with esprit de corps. Corporateness means that an organization, whether incorporated or not, takes on a life which is different from the sum of the activities and qualities of those individuals who are participating at any one time. Properly established, the organization provides for its own perpetuation through such mechanisms as membership practices, selection and rotation of leadership positions, funding and other maintenance systems. While many of the activities are carried out by individuals, the decisions about what those activities will be and why they are to be pursued will be made corporately, i.e., by a defined group be it membership, board or committee. The characteristics of corporateness are reinforced by the use of corporate job descriptions, provisions for stated and special meetings of each body, and quorum requirements.

The quorum is a good illustration of corporateness. If a certain kind of decision making is the board's responsibility and an issue in that category arises, a special meeting may be called. However, if only one or two people show up, they are not permitted to take action on behalf of the organization, except in the most extraordinary circumstances. The few that show up are not the board; they are only board members. The board itself is only deemed to exist when a stated portion, i.e., quorum, of the individual members has convened. Such a breakdown in attendance may suggest many urgent tasks which those individuals may properly pursue to get the organization on track but conducting a meeting and making a decision on the issue at hand are not among them.

These three developments--the division of labor, formalization of accountability and establishment of corporateness--are essential to the making of an organization which is going to be able to fulfill its mission. With each of these developments, the basic statements or POLICIES shaping the purpose, structure and modus operandi have been articulated. The work of the organization or OPERATIONS has been undertaken from these established reference points. This is a significant accomplishment and should be a source of great pride and pleasure for those individuals who have had a hand in it.

However, it marks significant and permanent changes in the relationship of individuals to the cause. No matter how you slice it, these changes involve the subordination of some individual autonomy to the will of the group and some restrictions on the nature and scope of any one person's involvement. Creation of a hierarchy means that some individuals by virtue of the positions they hold and not necessarily their charisma have access to more information and power than others. In the zealously individualistic, free wheeling, and often egalitarian atmosphere of volunteerism, such organizational facts of life seem particularly onerous.

As months, years and decades go by, the ongoing challenge becomes one of balancing the needs of the organization with those of the present and future members in such a way that the mission of the organization is being addressed. Experience suggests that in any workable organization, volunteer or not, the needs of individual participants must be understood and respected if the organization is to be successful. It is particularly incumbent on a volunteer organization which exists to address some concern related to human welfare, human dignity or social justice to treat its own personnel with dignity and fairness. Progress toward the stated goals of a volunteer organization will be little more than a pyrrhic victory if it has been achieved by treading on and otherwise abusing its individual members.

This general discourse on the nature of organizations and their development sets the stage for a more specific discussion of improving the effectiveness of those volunteers in the policy chain. To be sure, the specialization of tasks and formalized accountability directly affect all individuals in the organization whether policy or operations volunteer and whether they are volunteer or staff. Every niche filled reflects some kind of balance between organization and personal needs. For the policy volunteers, however, the corporateness factor has a special impact which varies depending on the volunteer's place in that chain.

6.2 OF BREAD AND BOARDS

6.2a Job Description: The Board of Directors

The board of directors is a corporate entity which in effect exists when it meets and when a quorum is present. Though a board is a collection of individuals, "it" has work which "it" must accomplish. The board's collective responsibilities generally include:

--establishing policies which govern the organization's programs, services, and administration

--monitoring the implementation of the existing policies and evaluating this information with an eye to

--planning and setting directions, goals, and objectives which not only meet legally mandated standards but which also further the organization's larger and longer-term purposes

--assuring that sound fiscal standards are maintained and that sufficient financial resources are secured to carry out all of the above. Or when the chips go down--as they have a way of doing--at least assuring that expenses mesh with available resources.

In some membership organizations the board's control and autonomy are restricted in certain areas. These are enumerated in constitutions and bylaws and frequently apply to membership standards, dues rates, and amendments to basic documents such as bylaws. However, in most volunteer groups, particularly those with large memberships or perhaps just an amorphous constituency, the board has full ultimate responsibility for the whole show and considerable latitude in shaping the performance and style of the organization. A board of this type is the governing body de jure; nearly every board governs de facto.

All of these elements are important, interrelated ingredients in policy making. However, the term policy-making may mislead those who expect it to resemble bread making. Some people seem to feel that policy, like bread, is best when made fresh daily, i.e., when they personally have had to vote on it at a given meeting. Yet even when the board does not establish a new policy per se, it has engaged in policy making by overtly or tacitly reaffirming the existing ones. A twenty-year old decision to affiliate with the local United Way or a century-old one to maintain membership in a national movement are policies which bind a present board. Unless there are compelling reasons to the contrary, these should be reaffirmed, and the current board's contribution be to assure that the organization is acting in accordance with any agreements involved. The only obviously new policy alternative, terminating those relationships, is probably foolish for the organization even if it would make individual board members feel like they had "done something." Ideally both new and reaffirmed policies reflect the best possible thinking about how the organization can fulfill its mission. They represent the optimum short- and long-term response which can be made at a given time.

Besides policy making, there are other collective functions which the board may be called on to perform. It may occasionally find itself serving as arbiter in personnel disputes which could not be resolved at lower levels of "appeal." This role is at the least a sticky wicket and can be distinctly unpleasant. However, it may be unavoidable and should prompt not only a decision about the case in point but also a review of existing policies and procedures. It should be determined if the issue reached the board partly because of sloppy personnel standards and practices and not just because of an interpersonal impasse.

Finally, in addition to using its collective wisdom to govern the internal workings of the organization, the board is expected to use its collective clout in the wider community to promote both the organization and the cause it serves. Often this role is exercised only in reaction to criticism. However, it can be a more positive, relationship-building one. Either way decisions about how, when, where and through whom the board's "voice" will be heard should be made consciously and collectively.

6.2b Job Description: Board Member

While the above job description is a legitimate summary of the work of the board itself, there is no getting around the fact that a board, however much it is a legal and functioning entity, is a collection of individuals who have been "hired" for a stated term through an election process. Much is expected of each of them individually. It is not as simple as "All you have to do is attend a few meetings." Duties include:

--understanding the job description of the board

--learning as much as possible about the organization including its history

--attending as many of the regular and special board meetings as humanly possible and arriving prepared, if materials have been sent in advance. (A corollary: notifying someone if you must miss an occasional meeting and resigning if absence becomes chronic)

--at the meetings, listening carefully and respectfully, participating in the discussion with observations and questions, and THINKING

--voting on the issues presented, keeping in mind that "no" is a legitimate vote. Abstaining only when absolutely necessary such as in a clear case of conflict of interest. In that event, make sure the abstention is carefully recorded

96

--interpreting the work of the organization to outsiders. Being its ambassador and presenting it in the most positive light possible. (Outside the board room, it is best to follow the advice Thumper received: If you can't say somethin' nice, don't say nothin' at all. To that we can add, if you can never find anything positive to say, you are in the wrong spot at the wrong time.)

--attending annual meetings or other corporate functions where the presence of board members is viewed as a demonstration of the board's active commitment.

In addition to these tasks which are common to members of all boards, some organizations expect the board members to serve on committees and to participate in formal fund-raising campaigns or projects. Some individuals will accept further specific assignments: being officers, chairing committees, or representing the organization at community or interorganizational functions. It is this writer's contention that where these additional tasks are routinely expected of every board member, they should be added to the job description when it is presented to prospective candidates. All too often they are tacked on later with a casual "Oh, by the way . . .." Otherwise, they should be viewed as jobs separate from regular board member duties and presented to the best candidate in a manner which conveys that the person may say no without being derelict in honoring the board membership commitment.

The fulfillment of these general duties takes more definite shape around the organization's substantive purposes. It is enriched by the various individual backgrounds, styles, opinions and areas of expertise contributed by members. While specific board positions may call for precise skills and qualifications, the consistent requirement for qualification is an understanding of the organization and willingness to participate fully in the corporate functioning of the board. Attending meetings is so essential that many bylaws permit a board to "fire" a member for frequent or chronic absence, if that absence is not well justified and/or disrupts the board's work. However, because the member has been elected, firing for this or any other

reason should be an absolutely last resort. The
esoteric phrase in many bylaws which permits a board to
remove a member "with or without cause" is jargon for
saying that the board does not necessarily have to go
public with its reason for ousting a member. For
example, if a member has mismanaged some funds, he/she
is rightly removed. Simply not liking someone is not
sufficient grounds and is not what is meant by "with or
without cause."

6.2c Key Persons

In a very real sense, every individual board member
is a key person and an equal partner to the others
around the table. After all, each has one vote. In
addition, a board will not have orderly and productive
meetings if only the president is paying attention to
the agenda or to parliamentary procedure. The board's
fiscal responsibility is not exercised if only the
treasurer can read the audit or financial statements. Nonetheless, certain persons, by virtue of the
positions they hold, are pivotal in determining whether
or not the collection of individuals is forged into a
collective force promoting the organization's effectiveness.

The NOMINATING COMMITTEE is a mechanism used by
most volunteer groups to assure that its top volunteer
positions are filled in a timely, systematic way with
qualified and committed persons whose individual skills
will benefit the organization and whose individual
attributes complement those of other board members. The
committee itself is sometimes selected by the board but
frequently is elected by the membership and accountable
to that body. In either case it is charged with
presenting a slate of candidates for regularly scheduled
elections and for providing recommendations to fill
vacancies which occur between elections.

It should go without saying that there is more to
the committee's job than filling slots with warm bodies
from among the friends of the committee. Yet that is
the spirit in which the task is often undertaken. To do
its job well, a nominating committee has to understand
fully the jobs of the board and its members. The

committee must analyze who is staying on the board to determine what skills and backgrounds are needed in the vacancies to keep board membership balanced and representative. It must comb the membership and constituency for all possible candidates, must select the most suitable candidates and the best grouping of qualified candidates, and then must sell the organization and the board job to those prospects. Thus, whether the subsequent election is a hot political one or a pro forma endorsement, the nominating committee plays a powerful role in defining the caliber of the board.

Once board membership is determined, other key volunteers take on specific responsibilities for assuring the effectiveness of the board and of its members. The PRESIDENT, for example, does more than preside at meetings, which itself is a challenge. He or she often has the stated authority to appoint committee chairpersons, to make other individual assignments, and to establish the agenda for board meetings, though good bylaws require ratification by the full board for many of these decisions. The president is called on to represent the organization and to speak for it at outside functions. By choosing to be a fearful figurehead or a fearless leader or a fair-minded facilitator, the president establishes a style which influences the entire operation. Good presidents appreciate the checks and balances attached to their position, understanding that they have plenty of room to put their own personal stamp on the organization without overturning all past decisions or controlling future ones. They can enjoy being a kingpin without having to be a queen bee, if you will pardon the mixed metaphor.

Most organizations make provision for an EXECUTIVE COMMITTEE whose membership consists of officers and specified board members such as key committee chairpersons or members-at-large. The purpose of an executive committee is to allow for a smaller and more easily convened group to be able to conduct some official business for the organization when action is required between board meetings. It may meet on call or at stated intervals. In regional, state, or national organizations, the expenses of having a full board meeting are a real factor. The legal authority of the executive committee and any limits on the action it may

99

take on the board's behalf are or should be clearly delineated in the bylaws. Usually an executive committee may not overturn an established policy nor can it authorize expenditures not consistent with an approved budget. However, beyond these the committee often serves as a valuable resource and "think tank" which works with the president in planning and implementing the short- and long-term work of the board. A board's job description is necessarily broad and ongoing; the executive committee can help refine it to address the issues and tasks which are most relevant at a given time. Judicious use of an executive committee can be invaluable; excessive use of it may undermine and usurp the role of the board.

Another key person in much policy volunteering is not a volunteer but the EXECUTIVE DIRECTOR whom the board has hired to administer the policies and programs it has approved. The executive serves "at the pleasure of the board." This quaint bylaws phrase has a whimsical ring which belies the seriousness with which a board does or had better do its hiring and, heaven forbid, its firing. Indeed the executive is rightly expected to conduct the day-to-day work of the organization in a manner consistent with the board's decisions, i.e., to implement policies, and to see that other staff do likewise.

However, the executive's relationship to policy making is not best viewed as a passive, after-the-fact response. By virtue of full-time investment in the organization and of professional expertise, the executive has perhaps the most complete picture of what is happening, what the ramifications of the board's decisions are, and what changes may be needed. The executive director thus has the obligation and the opportunity to provide the board with complete information so that it may assess agency functioning and understand where its policies need to be refined or changed. Furthermore it is the executive's prerogative to propose specific policy changes for the board's consideration. This is NOT the same thing as asking for the board's rubber stamp.

The power of the executive, though not parliamentary, is professional, political and very real. Whether docile or domineering or somewhere in between, the executive is a central figure in policy making, a kingpin in a very real sense. One problem which can arise is developing a healthy and positive working relationship between the executive and the other king-pin, the president, particularly if both want to be the queen bee. (This phenomenon is not gender-related.) It is always difficult to keep the two roles balanced and can be very disruptive to the organization if the people in these roles will not keep them balanced.

The last category of key volunteers who affect policy making are those who are appointed to the various committees. Since it is probably the largest numeri-cally, we will give it the courtesy of its own section in this chapter.

6.3 OF CAMELS AND COMMITTEES

Of all the mechanisms which can make or break policy volunteering, the committee is perhaps the most critical and the most criticized. Referring an item to committee evokes titters or sighs, as if this were an automatic death sentence for any issue. The tired joke about a camel being a horse designed by a committee captures the essence of the frustration many find with committee work. However, it does so without looking at the possibilities that a camel may be more useful than a horse in a given situation and that it is not ultimately the committee's fault if the camel is adopted where the horse would have been more appropriate.

6.3a Job Descriptions

In relation to policy-making, a committee, like a board, is a corporate entity and has many of the same collective obligations: monitoring programs, services, and administration; evaluating these in relation to the organization's goals and objectives; and developing policy positions which will enhance organizational functioning.

Unlike a board, a committee is focusing on one facet of the total operation and is not responsible for that total picture, though it helps if the committee has some insights into it. A committee is the board's specialist in a certain area. Any "final" policy-elated action of the committee is not final at all. It is made in the form of a recommendation to the board, where a proposal may be accepted, amended, rejected, or, alas, sent back to committee. In other words, while relying heavily on committee information and insights, the board retains the right to discard or disregard them altogether. This may sound foolish and often would be. Nonetheless, that is the way it is, and it is consistent with the formal legal accountability of the board, an accountability which does not apply to committee action.

Committees are unlike boards in another area. Most committee members and chairpersons are "hired" by being appointed by the president with board approval. The nominating and executive committees are exceptions; and some organizations elect other committees or at least the chairpersons of standing committees. This seemingly subtle hiring difference is important in emphasizing that most committees are creatures of the board itself and are its agents in the policy division of labor. Committee members, like the executive director, serve "at the pleasure of the board." The wise board chooses committee members carefully and then listens to what they say.

As the committee's corporate nature somewhat parallels that of the board, so does the job description for individual committee members resemble that of individual board members. The obvious exception is that when a committee member votes, it is not the last step in determining the outcome of a policy issue. Individual commitment, expertise, and willingness to learn are qualities as essential to effective committees as to effective boards. It may even take a little more imagination to be a committee member in order to remember how important the role is even though it is a subordinate one on the organizational charts.

In addition to policy functions, the committee member may be expected to participate in the implementation of decisions once they are made. Often they are in fact disappointed if they cannot. Few Ways and Means

Committees, for example, would not expect to have to work in some capacity on the bazaar or other project they had developed. The degree to which operational involvement by committee volunteers is appropriate is, of course, greatly determined by the type of committee, the type of organization, and the availability and assignments of paid staff. The only generally applicable statement which can be made is that the committee needs to have a clear distinction of its policy and nonpolicy functions and a clear delineation of the tasks related to each.

A final parallel between board and committee policy functions is that, in organizations with professional staff, the executive director or another staff member will serve as an associate providing information and ideas for the committee. The committee chairperson and the staff associate need to develop a good working relationship, and that presents the same challenges as the president/executive partnership.

6.3b Types of Committees

Committees come in many shapes and sizes, depending on the organization and its needs. They tend to fall in one of three categories. Of most ancient vintage is the STANDING COMMITTEE. The reason for having this type of committee is that there are some aspects of organizational functioning which require ongoing attention and that they are sufficiently complex as to require more detailed and time-consuming assessment than the board can give to them at its meetings. The theory is that a specialized group can develop the background and expertise which can be useful in developing policy alternatives and revisions for the board's consideration. Membership, finance, personnel, ways and means, program, public issues and building maintenance are a few examples.

Most standing committees have a job description laying around somewhere, unfortunately, often deep in the archives. Even with this document in front of it, a standing committee is more effective if it has in addition a specific charge from the board and/or a plan of work it has devised on its own. These give some focus to the committee's work within a defined time period. The standing committee, by virtue of its permanence, can provide for sustained development of organizational expertise in its area of concern. Through a careful rotation of membership, it can also provide for the introduction of new people and new ideas. It offers a golden opportunity to expand the base of committed and talented individuals beyond the membership of the board and can serve as a training ground for volunteer leaders. The gold tarnishes, however, if the committee is allowed to lose sight of its basic function and that function's particular relevance at a given time. If the truth were known, it is probably the misuse of standing committees which has given committees in general such a bad name.

The SPECIAL COMMITTEE is another device which boards and presidents can use to help them think through and deal with specific issues. When a topic does not fall under the purview of an existing committee and when it requires a highly concentrated expenditure of volunteer time and energy, a special committee may be just the ticket. To start with, there tends to be at least some thought given to why the committee will be created, what it will do, and by when its work will be completed. By design it goes out of existence when the task is completed. This fact makes it particularly attractive to individuals who have ever been trapped indefinitely on poorly managed standing committees or to those who are not able to assume a long-term responsibility. The special committee is often a good introduction to the organization for those whose expertise and newness might produce fresh insights on the problem at hand and whose satisfactory experience on the special committee might lead them to other involvement with the organization.

It is interesting and significant that these groups are rarely called by their proper parliamentary title. In an attempt to stress the shorter-term nature of the tasks and/or to add a little zip to weary nomenclature, it has become fashionable to call them ad hoc committees, task forces or even blue-ribbon panels. They remain, nonetheless, committees in terms of function and accountability. Regardless of how much the group's title, charge or membership glitters, the board retains final responsibility for the outcome.

The ADVISORY COMMITTEE is perhaps the most amorphous and most difficult to use effectively. Whether mandated (as in many government human service agencies) or not, many organizations find it useful to establish such a committee in order to have regular, sustained contact with key constituents. They often include past leaders and individuals representing some kind of community cross section from client group to community power structure. The resulting interaction produces feedback and insights which, if communicated to the board or public administrator, can help in assessing the organization's strengths and weaknesses.

Advisory committee members can also be ambassadors, interpreting the work of the organization in their spheres of influence. This gives an advisory committee considerable political value; but it must remember it has no parliamentary power. Neither a board nor an agency administrator is compelled to act on or react to any ideas coming from an advisory body. However, if an organization expects only unquestioning adulation of its work, it should re-examine its motives and decide if the advisory committee is worth anyone's time. From the individual's standpoint, the relatively few strings attached to membership on an advisory committee can be very appealing. An advisory committee is one place where putting your two cents in is the required task and you are not in danger of having to get deeply involved. It does not generally satisfy those who like to be "doing something."

Regardless of type, committees are not necessary evils. They are essential to the functioning of all but the smallest organizations. If properly developed and utilized, committees can be of great benefit to the organization and great personal satisfaction to the individual members.

6.4 CORROSION OF THE POLICY CHAIN

Throughout this rather generalized discussion of the different groupings of people in or near the policy chain, it has been impossible to avoid direct statements and inferences that, despite their logic and value, there are many points where effectiveness can break down or never even rear its head. Sometimes breakdowns occur simply because the individual participants--staff and volunteer--have never had organizational basics explained to them. So sloppy have we been that it is still possible for a volunteer to have held numerous policy positions without really understanding the policy function. In such cases the volunteer literature traditionally and correctly stresses the absolute necessity of good recruitment, training and orientation in order to assure at least minimum levels of knowledge. Yet organizations often fail to make the demands of time required for such activities. They either assume that everyone knows everything, or they are afraid to impose on already busy volunteers. Staff also need more training in their policy making role than they often get.

More ominous yet, it can and does happen that organizations and individuals who are sincerely con-cerned with their effectiveness and who devote consider-able time to those tasks which experience suggests will enhance it still find effectiveness elusive. Thus, before we identify some specific suggestions which ought to and probably will increase the effectiveness of policy volunteering, we need to examine some quiet forces which are constantly at work threatening to corrode the policy chain despite our best intentions and which this writer's experience suggests have been under-emphasized in the literature.

6.4a Forest vs. Trees Mentality

By its very nature, policy volunteering at any level is at least one step removed from the programs, services, and routine operation of the organization. At its most effective, policy volunteering is impersonal and objective. It is more abstract and hence less immediate in feedback than the kind of hands-on, "helping people" work usually associated with the word "volunteer." It requires the individual to maintain a certain distance from any one tree in order to assess the health of the entire forest (board) or of a particular species of tree (committee) and to assure the continued viability of the forest. Since the division of labor assigns different pieces of forest management to different individuals, each of them needs and has different information. More importantly, everyone does not need to know everything about everything in order for the work to proceed. In large organizations this is a good thing because no one could handle every last fact being generated.

One problem which arises is that people assigned tree duty develop an excessively possessive attitude. Instead of appreciating and caring for that tree as an integral part of the forest, they begin to believe that their tree is the only reason the forest exists. They begin to expect everyone to be as attentive to a new leaf as they are and to be jealous if they feel that a new pine cone has received more acclaim. Worse yet, someone else may get to make the decision that a tree must come down. Even if tree removal is essential to the health of the forest, the decision creates tension. NOTE: A tree tender has every right to make sure this is the real reason and every obligation to fight for the tree's preservation on those grounds.

For example, while serving as a board president, this writer was told by a staff member that it would be impossible for board members to do their jobs "properly" unless they served as part of the volunteer corps for her program. This direct service volunteer job required two hours a week. Aside from the fact that such a task was not in the board members' job description for good reason, this writer tried gentler explanations: The board was spending its time trying to solve the massive financial problems of that program so that it could be saved. The individual board members were committed to many weekly hours already. If this staff person's argument were valid, the same logic would compel direct service volunteering by board members in the five other major programs of the organization. All explanations fell on deaf ears. Unfortunately, many of the interpersonal tensions in this situation were never resolved. Fortunately, the structural and financial ones were, and a highly valuable community service was preserved.

At the other end of the policy spectrum from the zealous tree tender is a board whose members cannot personally examine every tree and who are constantly faced with the question of whether or not the information they get is sufficient and appropriate. Sometimes a board thinks it is looking at the actual forest, but it is really being shown a picture of the forest carefully painted by the executive or president to show it in its best light. If the board's response is an unquestioning "Fantastic!," it has no way of knowing if the real forest is healthy or if, though all looks fine at the moment, there is an invasion of gypsy moths on the way.

Other boards allow themselves to become overwhelmed and wearied by the complexity of the forest. Despite the best effort of the executive or president to present an accurate picture, board members prefer to look at one tree at a time, giving priority to the sick tree. This produces a crisis management approach to organizational problem solving which may head off short-term difficulties but rarely avoids long-term ones. As an illustration of how it is easier to comprehend a tree than a forest, watch different boards discuss agency budgets. Notice how many times it is the $100 expenditure rather than the potential $10,000 deficit which gets the most attention. Often it cannot even be argued that the former was either misspent in principle or is in fact part of the larger problem. That does not seem to matter.

In smaller organizations, particularly where there is no staff, it is even easier to focus on trees than forests. More people can and do know more details about the total operation. In addition, the policy volunteers are likely to be tree tenders as well as forest managers or are apt to be personal friends with the tree tenders. As a result, individual tree tenders may find it easier to gain access to the board and to feel that they have greater personal influence over the board's decisions. Even if they are right about this and are successful in saving the tree for now, this will not necessarily produce the hoped-for, long-term preservation of the forest.

If this forest/tree approach to describing personal perspectives seems simplistic or silly, it is no more so than many of the interpersonal squabbles and power struggles which occur when individuals at various points in or near the policy chain forget how important yet how limited each perspective is.

6.4b Groupthink

Personal blindspots and interpersonal tensions are closely related to some other group dynamics which are particularly relevant to decision-making groups. In looking for an explanation of how it happens that perfectly intelligent, presumably well-informed individuals can meet in groups to make what prove to be patently stupid and seemingly uninformed corporate decisions, psychologist Irving L. Janis analyzed group decision-making in high levels of government and observed a phenomenon he called "groupthink." According to Janis, groupthink is the "desperate drive for consensus at any cost that suppresses dissent among the mighty in the corridors of power" and the "development of group norms that bolster morale at the expense of critical thinking."[1] Groups carry this to the point of sticking to already established policies even though evidence that these are not working is available. So great are the individuals' desires for seeking concurrence, maintaining self-esteem, and promoting emotional equanimity that they drift into patterns of group behavior which encourage conformity and discourage dissent, disagreement and mere discussion of problems and alternatives. He describes the main principle of groupthink in the style of Parkinson's Law:

> The more amiability and esprit de corps there is among the members of a policy-making in-group, the greater the danger that independent critical thinking will be replaced by groupthink, which is likely to result in irrational and dehumanizing actions directed against outgroups.[2]

Groupthink promotes illusions of the invulnerability, inherent righteousness, and unanimity of the in-group. Its effect is so subtle that the group norms suppressing individual critical thought are internalized by each person so that each decides that any questions or concerns must not be relevant and should not be aired. Groupthink's most significant and insidious characteristic is its nondeliberateness. This makes it a slipperier process to deal with than other forms of group building and decision making.

While Professor Janis was looking primarily at the truly mighty in the corridors of power, groupthink occurs in the smaller hallways of policy volunteering. It may be even more difficult to combat in these arenas because the policies being made fall in that large gray area between the urgent decisions affecting the individual's well-being and those which will have immediate, public and global impact. When added to the general attitude that you should not ask too much of volunteers anyway, groupthink is both cause and effect of poor communication, sloppy or no planning and bad management at all points in the policy chain.

The need for a sense of in-groupness may produce a "you and me against the world" mentality within each category of personnel related to policy making: board vs. committee, committee vs. board, staff vs. volunteers. Or an organization anxious to demonstrate its concern for all the individuals in it may carry the "one big happy family" ideal to extremes. Some boards, for example, will rubberstamp almost anything on the grounds that the committee worked hard or the executive said so. Either position is counterproductive and destructive for the organization's larger purposes. Sooner or later groupthink will take its toll on the enthusiasm and satisfaction of the individuals involved. CAUTION: Not all cohesiveness and esprit de corps constitute groupthink. The line is hard to draw, but the major clues lie in assessing honestly what the impact of policy decisions has been on the organization's mission rather than on how good everyone felt about it.

6.4c The Bartholomew Cubbins Syndrome

Another factor dramatizing the inherent tensions between the corporate and individual facets of effective policy making has to do with the unique configuration of qualities, experiences and expertise which every person brings to a policy volunteering position. In a very real sense every individual has many hats, some of which will enhance his/her functioning in the organization and some of which will not. The challenges which this presents are not unlike those faced by Bartholomew Cubbins, a charming and well-intentioned Dr. Seuss character.[3] Bartholomew, according to the story, had removed his everyday hat to show respect for the king and did not realize that another had magically popped onto his head. When threatened with bodily harm if he did not bare his head, Bartholomew became painfully aware of the new hat and soon found himself tearing off hat after hat, unaware of where they were coming from but anxious to please the king.

Some "hats" cannot be changed, for they are not accessories at all but are characteristics of the individual. Age, sex, race, ethnicity, religion, social class and occupation are not easily checked at the door. Nor should they be. These characteristics only become "hats" within an organization if: (1) the individuals pick one of their own characteristics as The Hat they will wear or (2) as more often happens, they are perceived by others as having only one, perhaps two hats. The resulting tokenism, whether self- or group-imposed restricts the individual to viewing every concern from the perspective of that one character-istic. There is a substantial difference between knowing that a person's ideas are affected by age, sex, race, etc., and extrapolating from this that all people in a given category feel exactly the same way. For example, it does not necessarily follow that every utterance from the black, female member of the board has something to do with her being black or female. It certainly may, but it may not.

This particular hat problem is increasingly being brought to the attention of established organizations by outside groups. These outside groups recognize the importance of the policy-making function and understand the power inherent in it perhaps even more clearly at times than the policy makers themselves. They have observed quite correctly that some organizations and particularly their boards have become so homogenous, i.e., white, upper-class, male and/or management, that the resulting decisions are at the least limited in perspective and at worst unjust and unresponsive. These outsiders, i.e., minorities, low income, female and/or

111

labor, call for diversified representation on the boards of community service organizations and back up their demands with offers to provide qualified "representatives" for those boards.

This can be tremendously helpful to the organization which sincerely desires to be more open and diverse but which has become so ingrown it hardly knows where to begin. The move from homogeneity to tokenism to pluralism is never easy. However, unless the "representation" is formally defined and agreed to by all, it is inappropriate for one organization to attempt to control another by planting a mouthpiece or two on a board. It is equally inappropriate for an individual to undertake a policy-making position in one organization if his/her loyalties to another group will interfere with the full exercise of responsibilities in both. Just because these maneuvers may also describe with accuracy how existing boards got to be so homogenous, ingrown, and ineffective does not mean that fighting fire with fire is the effective remedy.

We have already mentioned other "hat" problems which arise within organizations. A particularly enthusiastic individual may perform a variety of functions for an organization either simultaneously or sequentially. Such a person must understand which hat is required, be that service volunteer, committee chair, or board member. Nominating committees need to remember that no one hat automatically qualifies a person for board membership or disqualifies either.

Different hats are not necessarily in conflict with each other, but they should be changed with the occasion. For example, committee chairpersons may feel that their job is to get the committee's recommendation passed by the board as presented and at any cost. However, at the board meeting, the discussion may produce questions and viewpoints which the committee did not consider. The board may take different action than the committee envisioned, and these committee chair/board members themselves may wish to see the recommendation amended or defeated. In fact they would be remiss as board members to settle for less than their best judgment when the board vote is taken. This does not need to be a no-win situation with the committee since many a committee will accept "defeat" gracefully when told the reasons for the board's actions. The committee may view its leader's change of heart as treason. Unfortunately, this is a personal risk which the wearer of more than one hat takes.

Currently in vogue is a new style of hat which is not confusing to the individual at all: self-aggrandizer. To be sure, this is not really a new hat. There have always been those who used such prestige and recognition as devolve from membership on certain boards and advisory committees for the sole purpose of adding to their own resumes. The new twist is that it is now fasionable to admit that you have this hat on and to justify wearing it by extolling the career development aspects of volunteering. Again it is a question of balance, for it would be dishonest to deny the status appeal of many board positions. However, the true self-aggrandizer is so busy looking out for number one that he/she will probably never carry a full share of the load. Even with an illustrious name to add to the letterhead, the self-aggrandizer will not be an effective board member.

The Bartholomew Cubbins story ends happily with the lad's five-hundredth hat being so beautiful that the king buys it for himself, leaving the boy bareheaded and the king in control. The happy ending for volunteer organizations is not producing bareheaded, obeisant subjects. It is rather to have individuals wearing appropriate hats and not being forced to wear either none at all or the same one for all occasions. Policy volunteering will be more effective if the organization is structured to enjoy a profusion of hats, with all the individual styles and colors implied and without sacrificing all sense of organizational stability and accountability.

6.4d Legal Ramifications

These interpersonal and group dynamics which threaten to corrode the policy chain have legal ramifications which policy volunteers and their staff associates need to appreciate without succumbing to fear and paranoia. As noted early on, boards of directors are the legally accountable bodies in incorporated organizations. This means that directors may be individually as well as collectively responsible for decisions made. In times past directors of charitable and religious organizations were assumed to be well-intentioned guardians of the public trust as that trust was invested in their private voluntary efforts. They were rarely called to task in a court of law. If that did happen, they could expect to be given the benefit of the doubt.

However, this may be changing in these times of the closed-in frontier. Directors may find themselves threatened with law suits and may learn the hard way that "meaning well" is not by itself sufficient defense. Boards and directors are being more closely scrutinized for three kinds of poor performance:[4]

Mismanagement--failure to exercise ordinary and reasonable care in the performance of duty exhibiting honesty and good faith

Nonmanagement--permitting negligent mismanagement by others to go unchecked

Conflict of interest--self-dealing which, though not absolutely barred, requires full disclosure and the closest scrutiny to determine if a duty or loyalty has been violated.

If these ring a bell in relation to forest/tree mentalities, groupthink, and Bartholomew Cubbins, that is good. While these are not precise parallels, it should be clear that the best legal defense may well lie in making every effort to overcome the obstacles to effective policy volunteering which these dynamics represent. Insurance protection, which will be discussed in Chapter 8, may ease the minds of individual directors. However, it does not excuse directors from keeping their management obligations clearly in view. An understanding of the legal ramifications may also help committees and staff who may not like to have their work and ideas "questioned" be a bit more tolerant of a questioning or critical board. Properly viewed, the legal dimensions increase the importance of every role in the policy chain rather than relieving anyone from the serious tasks required.

6.5 STRENGTHENING THE POLICY CHAIN

Moving from the abstract to the more specific, we will conclude this discussion of policy volunteering with some suggestions for steps which should improve its effectiveness. They are presented in chart form to show their relevance to the factors we have been discussing. You will quickly observe that the lists are neither complete nor original. The use of charts is not an attempt to disguise this but rather to emphasize that while we already know "how to," we may have forgotten "how come." If this chapter has done nothing more than refresh our memories about why and where we need policy volunteering, it has been useful. If it has added to our sense of urgency regarding effective policy volunteering as a top priority, so much the better.

Policy volunteering is not only essential to organizational functioning; it has the potential of offering individuals some of the most exciting, constructive and rewarding experiences they can ever have. The corporate and individual accomplishments which it permits can be absolutely astounding. In volunteer circles which believe there is more to be done about human welfare, human dignity and social justice, it is essential to unleash the full potential of policy volunteers.

REFERENCES

[1] Irving L. Janis, "Groupthink," PSYCHOLOGY TODAY, November, 1971, p. 43.

[2] IBID., p. 44.

[3] Theodor Seuss Geisel, THE 500 HATS OF BARTHOLOMEW CUBBINS (New York: The Vanguard Press, 1938).

[4] Paul C. Gouldin, LET THE TRUSTEE BEWARE (Binghamton, N.Y.: Levene, Gouldin and Thompson, 1979), p. 3.

STRENGTHENING THE POLICY CHAIN

I. Getting the Corporate House in Order

FORMALIZED ACCOUNTABILITY

Review all basic documents: Articles of Incorporation, constitution, bylaws, agreements with funding sources or parent groups.

Know where the originals are, and circulate copies.

Use parliamentary procedure.

Keep complete records.

Have a regular plan for reviewing all existing policies and affiliations.

Have a regular plan for reviewing the organization's compliance with applicable laws.

CORPORATENESS

Understand the basic documents.

Compile a policy manual which summarizes existing policy. Consider a looseleaf format to facilitate updating.

Use agendas, preferably written and mailed in advance.

Develop organization work plans annually.

Be working on long-range plans for next 3-5 years. Involve many in this process and circulate results widely within organization.

DIVISION OF LABOR

Review bylaws.

Make sure required positions are filled and functioning.

Update all job descriptions and committee work plans.

NEVER use a special committee to do a standing committee's job unless all other attempts to use standing committee have failed, including giving it all new members.

Make sure that nomination and election procedures are in place and assure both rotation and continuity.

II. Maximizing Individual Inputs

FOREST/TREES

Orient all staff and volunteers to policy function and structure.

Assure two-way communication from board to committee, board to staff.

e.g., Invite committees to submit interim informational reports enroute to a policy recommendation.

Involve staff in evaluating impact of policy alternatives on operations.

Explain decisions where possible.

Encourage regular meetings of board and standing committees. "On call" encourages crisis management.

Plan ahead and make good use of those regular meetings.

GROUPTHINK

Encourage discussion. Invite questions. Allow time for this in agenda.

Whenever possible, consider policy alternatives.

Understand the intent of parliamentary procedure and USE IT.

When taking a vote, allow time for people to respond when it is time to vote "no."

Use written reports, preferably mailed in advance.

Use "outside" help (consultants, advisory committees) for a shot in the arm.

Get well enough acquainted to appreciate differences without getting clubby.

BARTHOLOMEW CUBBINS

Have year-round plan for recruitment, training, and placement of policy volunteers.

Require participation in orientation as a condition of selection or election.

Develop ongoing education plan. e.g., Take 5-10 minutes at each meeting to review a background item even if it is not on the agenda for action.

If people persist in mixing up their hats, discuss it openly or try group exercises which address this problem.

Do not use policy positions as rewards for years of service in operations.

7

THE OPERATIONS VOLUNTEERS

7.1 THE MANY FACES OF OPERATIONS VOLUNTEERING

At last we have arrived at the point of discussing those activities which are widely perceived as the heart of volunteerism. We are talking about the countless invididual acts of commitment encompassing an endless variety of volunteer tasks:

Being a friendly visitor or Big Brother/Sister
Serving as a Scout leader or youth group advisor or coach
Giving parties at nursing homes
Answering a hotline phone and offering crisis counseling

Licking stamps and doing clerical work for a worthy
cause
Making speeches or posters for a cause
Serving as a school, library or hospital aide
Providing transportation for the aged or handi-
capped
Running bake sales and bazaars
Soliciting $1 per household for a health drive
Soliciting $10,000 gifts for a major capital
campaign

We are talking about doing good and meaning well in the
very best sense these phrases can imply. Any complete
listing of the different ways in which they manifest
themselves could be a book in itself.

We are also focusing this part of our discussion on
those volunteer tasks being performed in an organizational context. We will continue on the premise that
there are common threads which need to be woven into our
understanding of who the volunteers are and what they
do. This requires pulling back from warm cozy images
and taking a cold hard look. This was somewhat easier
to do with policy volunteering because by definition the
work is more abstract. By nature the organizational
structures in which it takes place have more in common
with each other than seems to be the case in the myriad
of settings where operational services are performed. It was also easier because popular opinion
tends to translate the more abstract, impersonal,
corporate and objective facets of policy making to mean
that policy volunteers themselves are aloof and
uncaring. Thus there is less resistance to describing
them in categorical ways. As we have seen, this
attitude is an inaccurate description of many, perhaps
even most, individuals who serve with dedication and
concern as policy volunteers. It is also counterproductive in understanding the organizational functions and
personal factors which enhance or detract from assuring
that operations volunteers are helping an organization
carry out its task of providing service.

In the discussion of policy volunteering we
examined different individual and corporate "jobs" which
have a place under that general heading. The structures
and functions are the same regardless of the subject

matter of the organization. Despite the greater diversity of tasks and job titles, it is quite possible and productive to do this for operations volunteering as well. Note: We will concentrate on volunteers already at work in existing organizations, leaving the bulk of our discussion of recruitment until Chapter 9. The reason for this is that we have plenty of problems using the ones we do have which cannot be "blamed" on recruitment.

7.1a People Helping People

DIRECT SERVICE is a rather crisp term describing the kind of individual caring and sharing associated with good old-fashioned neighboring. As such it carries on a long tradition of active charitable concern which encompasses attempts by one person to ease physical and mental suffering of others and/or to enrich the quality of life of the persons perceived to be in need through "hands-on, face-to-face" intervention by the individual volunteer/good neighbor. It is helpful to view direct service as a form of extended neighboring but only if we can separate myth from reality in our images of neighboring.

First, while there have apparently always been individuals who were concerned about others and wanted to or thought they should express that concern immediately and tangibly, the form of their actions has been shaped by:

--religious and secular definitions of who one's neighbors are and how they are to be treated

--the degree to which a given condition was perceived as a problem which could be solved rather than as an inevitable fact of life

--the state of scientific and technical knowledge about causes and treatments

--the availability of other forms of help.

Help was given and received in a social context and on terms beyond those defined by the two parties.

Secondly, the appealing mental picture of people helping people glosses over the reality that one person, however concerned, can only help so many others or can only do so much to help any other person. The most we can expect is that a volunteer/good neighbor can help some of the people some of the time. Choice of how, when or whom to help will vary with the volunteer's perception of the problem and his/her personal capacity and resources for responding. Neighboring is no more and no less than an optimum response by some people to some needs at some times. It is not automatically dispensed with any more caring and compassion than welfare from the worst modern bureaucracy. If it had been ultimately effective in meeting all perceived needs, we would not have seen the development of our crazy quilt of human services. These were created at least as much because caring persons wanted to exercise social responsibility as because indifferent ones wanted to abdicate it. The establishment of service organizations allowed and allows for extended neighboring by those who wish to be directly involved. It represents another optimum response for some needs some of the time.

The decision to do any sort of neighboring/direct service has the potential of giving the volunteer a substantial and immediate sense of personal satisfaction and accomplishment. In our large, complex, mobile society, it may permit individuals to combat depersonalization and fragmentation in their own lives as well as those of the clients. Whether the service involves a crisis/survival need or a life-enrichment one, the volunteer can see first hand the impact of helping. By the same token, the immediacy of feedback brings risks of knowing failure and frustration. Among these are client "ingratitude," seeing need greater than any one person can address, or feeling like one has a finger in a crumbling dike.

Out of the veritable smorgasbord of worthy causes, volunteers consciously or unconsciously choose those organizations which best express their perceptions of needs and appropriate responses. The confines of the organization can do several positive things for the individual volunteer:

--Validate the legitimacy of the volunteers' perceptions at least to the extent of assuring them that they are not the only ones who believe that the needs exist and can be addressed. This also validates the underlying reality that it is okay to address some needs even if you cannot do everything.

--Connect the volunteers with the persons in need. This is especially important in our times where the perceived needs inspiring volunteer involvement may not manifest themselves next door but thanks to modern communications, one can certainly know they exist.

--Provide mechanisms and procedures which help the volunteer match concern with appropriate responses, i.e., a definition of how to help. It may mean making available such modern technology as sophisticated telephone systems for hot lines and computerized information and referral systems.

--Assure the volunteer that efforts will be made to promote continuity in meeting the perceived needs when the limits of individual time, energy and commitment are reached. (This is not necessarily equivalent to licensing the volunteer to drift in and out whimsically.)

--Provide networks within the organization and between organizations for sharing successes and failures, for pooling information and resources, and perhaps even improving the quality of response.

However, the organizational confines serve functions other than supporting the volunteers and their good intentions. The primary one is or should be to meet client needs. For example, some self-help groups are based on the premise that the best help comes from other persons who are suffering from the same problem. Other groups such as hospices for the terminally ill believe that too recent an experience with terminal illness may interfere with the volunteer's ability to work with others now experiencing it. In both cases, unbridled sympathy is deemed inappropriate. If that is the volunteer's only asset, there will not be a fit.

A second function of the organization's confines is to meet needs in those substantive areas and in accordance with those policies established as appropriate for the organization. Compliance with these may make the volunteers feel like both victims and perpetrators of the fragmentation, bureaucracy, pseudo-professionalism, and depersonalization they are trying to combat. Sometimes they are absolutely right. Other times this assessment is unduly harsh, if not entirely wrong. To illustrate, Meals-on-Wheels programs are created to provide nutritious meals to the homebound, usually with the added bonus of providing personal contact with the individuals so isolated. Common sense and health department regulations require that hot food arrive hot and cold food cold to avoid spoilage and contamination. This means that the volunteer delivery person had better not feel so sorry for the first recipient on the route and chat so long that the delivery schedule is delayed and other recipients' health jeopardized.

In a less dramatic case, adults who volunteer to be Scout or other youth leaders often feel they are performing well if they show up regularly. They forget that the organization is based on the premise that a certain need, e.g., character development, is addressed through certain sequences of activities. Uninformed, untrained leaders who see the job as entertaining the kids or who use the leadership position to barrage the youth with their personal accomplishments and ego needs may not do any real harm. Neither will they do much good except to add to the organization's statistics.

It is a value judgment by the individual volunteer and the organization as to whether the benefits of the service outweigh the drawbacks of the organizational confines. Is optimum better than nothing? Are we at optimum or minimum? These are good questions, but they are not best answered by flagrant disregard of procedures by well-intentioned volunteers.

Another type of operations volunteer engaged in actual performance of a service which an organization exists to provide is the ADVOCATE. The needs advocacy volunteers see are often similar to those perceived by direct service volunteers such as hunger, family breakup and emotional distress. However, advocates see these needs as affecting a group of people and being caused at least in part by the failure of social organizations and institutions to respond meaningfully. Therefore, the advocacy volunteers believe that their involvement should be at a systems level instead of an individual one. Rather than filling in the cracks by interpersonal involvement, they choose to try to repair the cracks and strengthen the basic structure of the systems affecting the perceived problems. Advocates engage in such activities as promoting public awareness and support of a given cause, lobbying legislators, monitoring public and private administrative agencies, testing issues through court cases and testifying at public hearings. These activities are targeted primarily at the policy and administrative decision makers who shape existing organizations and who, therefore, can presumably reshape them or create new ones, given sufficient public demand and support. Advocates believe that such realignments will have a positive, more long-range and hence more effective impact on the needs perceived.

While direct service is often favorably compared to neighboring, advocacy volunteering is suspect because of its association with politics. Advocacy is political by nature, though in a broader sense and on more levels than that word usually implies. Partisan politics which concentrates on getting candidates of a given political party elected is certainly a long-standing channel for American voluntary activity. When an individual's commitment to a particular political party is based on convictions that the general philsophy, specific platform and/or past performance of that party will best address perceived needs regarding human welfare, human dignity and social justice, participation in partisan politics is a form of volunteer work as we have defined it.

At another level advocacy focuses on an issue or set of issues and is nonpartisan, concentrating on activities for the enactment and administration of laws related to the performance of the public sector. The controversial Equal Rights Amendment is a case in point with much advocacy volunteering on all sides. Other advocacy extends to any and all fronts where action on the issue would improve society's total response. A community mental health organization may offer educational programs to individuals and may promote changes in personnel services in private industry as well as support legislative changes.

Anyone can stand on a soapbox and promote a cause. Most advocacy volunteers find it advantageous to work in an organization for all the same reasons direct service volunteers do. Particularly because advocacy's aim is to make a dent in larger systems, the organization with its constituency and structural continuity increases the likelihood that some impact will be made. Sometimes success is achieved quickly; other times the struggle is long and hard. If a round is lost or if the closing of one crack creates new ones in other parts of the same system, as it often does, the individual advocacy volunteer who has given all to one struggle may be comforted to know that there are others to carry on.

Even if their entire thrust is advocacy, organizations set limits on both the subject matter they will pursue and the techniques they will use. These limits may be self-imposed to help increase the organization's effectiveness and its credibility on a given issue over a period of time. The limits may also be imposed on an organization by virtue of its legal status. For example, if it has been chartered as nonpartisan, formally endorsing specific candidates is a violation of the terms of incorporation even though it is clearly a viable means of making a dent in a system. If the group's primary mission is to provide a charitable or educational service, certain service-related advocacy activities such as lobbying are permitted but only within limits of time and dollars defined by tax laws as interpreted by the Internal Revenue Service. Noncompliance may jeopardize the organization's tax-exempt status.

Most of these limits are not nearly as restrictive as some organizations have tried to make them out. Advocacy-oriented volunteers who believe that the organization's services will be enhanced by advocacy may appropriately test and refine their advocacy skills by convincing the organization to become more involved in the "political" arena. However, when the volunteer's perception of which advocacy stone must be turned does not mesh with that of the group, the volunteer must either look elsewhere or accept the organization's definition and work within it. Once again, "optimum" is the issue.

7.1c Helping People Help People and Save Humanity

Large numbers of volunteers perform tasks which have nothing direct to do with helping people. They are involved with the care and feeding of organizations or ORGANIZATIONAL MAINTENANCE. This form of "doing good" is predicated on the assumption that the organization being maintained is addressing human needs which the individual volunteer believes are urgent and valid.

Much organizational maintenance volunteering is best described as HOUSEKEEPING, the performing of routine tasks necessary to keep the organization functioning. They are seldom glamorous and are often downright drudgery when viewed as isolated pieces of work: typing, stuffing envelopes, making and distributing posters, rolling bandages, keeping records, managing supplies, doing bookkeeping and the like. They may require high level skills or virtually none at all. Since the feedback on how much good these tasks are doing does not come from the front lines of the organization's activities, these volunteers often look for and deserve to find satisfaction in being told why they really do make a difference and in having pleasant surroundings and relationships with co-workers. In other words, organizational housekeeping may appeal to volunteers as much for its fellowship and recreational aspects as for its generalized usefulness. It can be offered as valuable to the organization on these terms. On the other hand, these volunteers are taking less risk of personal failure regarding the human needs being addressed. They need to remember that a clean, well-organized house does not make a "home" and that there are limits to how inherently gratifying housework can be, however essential. Sometimes it just has to be done.

Closer to the front lines are SUPPORT volunteers who work with the direct service or advocacy volunteers rather than with the clients or target audience. Included in this category are recruiters, trainers, co-ordinators, researchers and speech writers. These volunteers often come from the front lines. This may be for a simple change of pace, but it is likely to happen because their perception of need has expanded to include appreciation of the fact that real do-gooding requires volunteers who are appropriately prepared and placed. The support volunteers engage in hands-on tasks which require an understanding of the organization, its potential and its limitations; a sensitivity to the needs of clients or issues and the needs of volunteers; and the ability to mesh all these. The support tasks generally require a high degree of skill, the use and development of which can be very rewarding to the volunteer. When they actually produce more effective front-line volunteers, satisfaction for the support volunteers increases. Like the housekeepers, support personnel must live with the vicarious assurance that service has improved as a result of their efforts and with the understanding that their role may never get the attention it deserves.

Up front but in a different arena of action are the FUNDRAISING volunteers for whom there surely must be a special place in heaven. While love and concern for humanity may make the world go round, money helps lubricate the wheels. Most human service organizations operate on a shoestring or think they do. They rely heavily on volunteers to raise money. Like other organizational maintenance volunteers, fundraisers operate on the assumption that the organization is performing useful services or promoting a worthy cause and that their volunteer services will ultimately mean that more work is done better.

Even when these are correct assumptions, the committed fundraiser has to struggle to hang on to this conviction in the face of the hard work involved in every kind of fund raising. Asking people to part with their hard-earned money can be one of the touchiest, most threatening tasks a volunteer can undertake. For one thing, the volunteer can identify with John and Jane Q. Public's frustration with the nonstop parade of worthy causes needing money and may be timid about adding to that frustration. Sometimes the process can be made more palatable to donor and solicitor by attaching an exchange of goods and services. Hence, the bake sale, the bazaar, the raffle, the charity sports tournaments, etc., etc., and so forth. Other activities currently in vogue offer the donor the opportunity to support a cause "only" if a volunteer fundraiser (usually a young person) "earns" it. Thus, the (Fill-in-the-blank)-a-thon in which the donor agrees to pledge so much per unit of performance by the volunteer. Collecting pledges before and money afterward can be as grueling as the ten-mile walk.

There comes a time when the only reasonable fundraising alternative is to ask straight out for a pledge or a donation, a feat which many individuals find does not come naturally. Proper preparation, good training, a clear understanding of duties and deadlines and lots of moral support are essential if the volunteer is to withstand the rigors of fundraising. Of course, it can also be tremendously gratifying, particularly if a goal is reached or surpassed.

From the organization's point of view, good fundraising can generate not only much needed dollars but also considerable goodwill among its constituency. It can heighten awareness of the organization in the community at large. This means that the organization's fundraising decisions will include selecting activities in keeping with the nature of the organization and pursuing those which seem most productive for dollar and public relations reasons. Having done this, the organization must protect itself and its credibility by requiring strict accountability from individual fundraisers and by curtailing excesses of the overzealous. A distortion of the organization's case which borders on false advertising or the use of strong-arm tactics which take the "voluntary" out of voluntary giving may generate a few dollars for the current project or campaign. However, sooner or later the organization pays too high a price for such gifts. It can neither afford nor be expected to tolerate individuals' bad performance on the grounds that they meant well.

Understanding this functional typology and applying it are helpful first steps toward improving the effectiveness of operations volunteering. The organizational setting both facilitates and limits many forms of meaning well. There must be a conscious, consistent and continuous reconciliation of individual and organizational needs.

7.2 FLAWS IN THE OINTMENT

Recognizing that volunteers bring different perceptions and perform different functions in the organizations they serve is certainly more useful than lumping them all into a faceless category. Some of the discrepancies between individual and organizational expectations can be reconciled by greater clarity and precision from both parties. However, there are other factors at work which warrant closer attention.

7.2a Lady Bountiful Revisited

Perhaps the biggest shock wave to hit volunteering in recent years is the presumed disappearance of women from the ranks of volunteering. Additional force was given to this shock wave by the public statements of some feminist leaders that volunteering exploits women by reinforcing their status as economic dependents, by keeping them busy and out of the work force (i.e., the real world), and by excluding them from decision-making circles even within many volunteer organizations.[1] Now that the dust has settled a bit, some curious and significant developments can be noted which had been obscured because of the stranglehold Lady Bountiful had on our images of volunteers.

First of all, it is probably not true that women have disappeared from volunteering. ("Probably" was inserted because of the problems of counting which are discussed in Appendix B.) It is probably more accurate to say that many of the women who volunteer are demanding participation in the full spectrum of volunteer opportunities and are no longer willing to be restricted to direct service and organizational maintenance work. You will recall from Chapter 3 that these were the activities outside the home which were considered ladylike extensions of womanly concerns and which came to be the activities considered "volunteering." Policy making within voluntary organizations and politically-oriented advocacy were largely perceived as men's work and were called doing one's civic duty. This sex-based division of volunteer labor has carried over to the present[2] and has even reared its head in modern social movements such as civil rights for blacks.[3]

It not only shows up in the relative proportions of men and women in policy volunteering but also in the paths by which each is likely to arrive at policy positions. In a Fortune magazine article entitled "Some Executives' Wives Are Executives Too,"[4] the volunteer careers of several women showed years of direct service and organizational maintenance work preceding the top leadership position. Though the article did not offer a comparison with their male counterparts, it does raise the question about how the men "earned" their positions. Closer to home, this writer met a relative newcomer to the community whose past volunteer experience and documentable achievement lay clearly in the realm of policy volunteering and particularly long-range planning. She had lived in the area long enough to have identified an organization which captured her imagination and commitment and in the best style of the professional volunteer, submitted a resume to that board's nominating committee for consideration. She was told in no uncertain terms that her overture was inappropriate and that if she really wanted to be on the board, she should show her commitment by leading children's tours for the institution. The same activity was apparently not considered essential for a new male bank official with less residence time whose name was on the ballot. Women are being urged to break these cycles and to abandon traditional volunteer roles. Many women are doing just that, and their desertion of those ranks has been noticed.

If women are volunteering less, there are practical as well as philosophical reasons. More women--numerically and proportionately--are employed outside the home. Many take jobs out of economic necessity; others pursue careers for status, self-fulfillment and other reasons. After hours, employed women with families are still carrying the major responsibility for housework and childcare. Some women who are not employed outside the home have their hands full with home and childcare responsibilities for which hired help is seldom available even if one can afford it.

Even those who most closely resemble the Lady Bountiful stereotype--upper-middle-class housewives whose children are in school all day or are grown and gone--may not choose volunteering as an outlet. While they may have considerable discretionary time, they have more options and resources for the use of it. They are quite tired of being taken for granted in volunteering as well as in other facets of their lives. They resent having it assumed that they will take up the slack left by those who have made other choices.

Any way you look at it, these changes in women's lives mean that there are fewer women with great gobs of unclaimed leisure time who are willing to volunteer indiscriminately for every worthy cause which presents itself. Unfortunately many volunteer programs particularly but not exclusively those serving youth in and after school are based on the assumption that this amorphous pool of volunteers exists. They have not adapted their approaches to deal with the realities of who is available and when.

The Lady Bountiful approach to the use of volunteers has been extended to other groups of volunteers who are extraneous to the work force: retired people and youth. Granted, these are indeed people who may have discretionary time, and it makes sense to tap all volunteer sources. However, our use of volunteers from these groupings is often overlaid with an attitude of amazement that such individuals do in fact have something to offer, given their irrelevance to the real world. This has led to an extension of the kid glove, china doll handling of volunteers which was inspired by

Lady Bountiful and which remains patronizing and demeaning when laid on with a trowel.

On the bright side, despite this new emphasis on policy making and advocacy as the "in" forms of volunteering, there is considerable direct service and organizational maintenance volunteering going on even in feminist circles. For example, the same groups of women who denounced "volunteering" have established hot lines, counseling centers, and emergency housing services. They hold rummage sales and other rather traditional forms of fund raising. The difference is not then in the tasks they are willing to do but rather the causes for which they are willing to do them. The original feminist complaints about sex discrimination in volunteering are well-founded. The subsequent feminist response has, however, reinforced rather than renounced the historically consistent patterns of who volunteers and why. Both have helped those of us who will let it shake us out of old stereotypes.

7.2b Supplementing/Supplanting Staff

Almost as touchy as the women's issue is that of staff/volunteer relationships. In organizations which have paid personnel this takes a special toll on the operations volunteers because they are the ones directly involved on what has come to be viewed as staff turf: carrying out activities which fulfill the mission defined in the policy chain. Much to the pride and relief of volunteers past, many services once provided exclusively by volunteers are now the province of professionally trained staff and other paid personnel. This leaves present volunteers in various dilemmas. An oft-quoted, shorthand definition of staff/volunteer roles is that volunteers supplement rather than supplant staff. This phrase makes a certain amount of sense and sounds innocent enough. However, it has a few kickers in it which need to be understood.

"Supplementing" staff implies that the ideal is to have human services provided by trained, paid personnel who work full-time and "know what they are doing." Second best is to use paid paraprofessionals and nonprofessionals under professional supervision.

Having to use volunteers to help out is the last resort, a necessary evil, and/or an admission of failure on someone's part to secure adequate levels of professional recognition and community support. As the division of labor within service fields increased, as different pieces of the action were assigned according to skill levels required, and as the notion of "team" was introduced to clarify working relationships among staff, volunteers were thought of as leftovers to be worked in and around as necessary. In addition we have assumed that volunteers cannot be required to participate in orientation and training which will help them understand their roles, how they fit into the total picture, and where their activities are restricted and why. It is small wonder then that many volunteers are indeed under foot.

A related problem has been that staff training does not include sufficient emphasis on how to incorporate volunteers into service teams, though there is plenty of printed material on this subject and plenty of practical evidence that volunteers will be part of the job scene. Where such emphasis is given, it is frequently targeted at the top professional and administrative staff who, it is to be hoped, are more attuned to planning, supervision and other people-management concerns than subordinate staff but who may forget to share this information with all staff who interface with volunteers.

As we can see from the previous section of this chapter, the difference between some volunteers and some staff is not necessarily in the tasks they do but in the amount of time they have agreed to spend doing them for the organization. In these tasks the volunteers do supplement staff by increasing the number of hands available to accomplish necessary work.

Some activities, especially those in direct service, are appropriately assigned to professionally trained personnel. Many forms of therapy, medical care and education impact such crucial areas of individuals' lives that the client/patient/student has the right to know that the helping person has the necessary qualifications. Yet there may be components of even these areas which are enhanced by enlightened and committed

volunteer efforts. For example, a teacher could tutor a
slow learner if he did not have responsibility for the
other twenty-nine students. A volunteer aide can also
help that child learn what the teacher is teaching,
given the tools and the training. A caseworker in a
nursing home has the same time problem in chatting with
residents and their families; and a volunteer can
augment the services provided by listening to the
rambling recollections of a lonely patient.

Use of volunteers may "supplement" by adding
flexibility to the availability of services and extend-
ing the geographic area served. By virtue of their NOT
doing a job full-time, volunteers can sometimes bring a
freshness and enthusiasm which is hard to maintain day
in and day out.

Because of the "politics" and persuasion involved
in advocacy and fund raising, it is more appropriate to
view staff as supplementing these volunteers. Much of
the up-front, public work in these areas is most effectively done by volunteers with staff providing the
support data and developing the materials.

"Supplanting" is a somewhat different
story. Potential for supplanting ranges from subtle to
blatant. On the subtle end of the scale, fogginess in
defining how and when volunteers can effectively mesh
with staff may be combined with other factors such as
bureaucratic demands, large caseloads/classes, and other
time-consuming uses of staff. This may result in the
volunteer providing what strikes the clients as the
human touch and leading to their bestowing affection and
respect only on the volunteer. More to the point, it is
often easy for the volunteer to identify and sympathize
with client needs, to get the positive feedback, and to
intentionally or unintentionally take all the credit for
having done the good deeds. Some carry this to the
extreme of feeling superior to the mindless, heartless
"they" in the office. Staff who had thought they would
have these direct contacts with clients may resent being
confined and undervalued.

If the volunteer's staff contacts are unwilling
(because of professional frustration and jealousy), if
they are unable (due to insufficient skill) to

communicate with the volunteers, or if there is little structured contact at all, the volunteers will be tempted to adopt this stance. They may forget that it was the organization and its staff's concern for client well-being which brought them together in the first place and which supports them when feedback is negative or the going gets rough. If volunteers are not included as part of the team, they may adopt an attitude of knowing how to do everyone's job. This defense mechanism is not, by the way, the exclusive province of volunteers. It happens with many people who have ideas and concerns but no channel through which to express them.

Sometimes "supplant" is thought to mean preventing the creation of paid positions. This may be true in a given instance for a short period of time. However, the historical record shows that the involvement of volunteers often leads to the creation of positions.

Closely related and more threatening is the implication that a volunteer will take away a job once held by staff. There lurks the notion that many staff positions can be terminated without too much trouble because volunteers would and could be rushed in to take over. This alternative is frequently kicked around by boards and the general citizenry when money gets tight, though few of these folks consider themselves part of this eager and available pool of volunteers.

Unquestionably a money crunch produces a substantial upheaval which may result in some staff positions being terminated. Moreover, paid positions may be realigned or abandoned for other management reasons than lack of money. One is that a particular job is no longer relevant to the organization; another that pieces of a current job are still important but the total position is more of an investment than is required. Hard as this is on the jobholder, termination may be a necessary and wise decision. It should have nothing to do with volunteers. Sometimes money shortages and the alleged availability of volunteers are inappropriately used to justify a retrenchment which is actually a coverup for removing an incompetent employee.

If any volunteers are to be "blamed" for the loss of paid positions, it is those policy makers who may not have done everything they could to assure adequate financial support. Yet even those who do knock themselves out may get caught in circumstances beyond their control. In either event, it is not the average operational volunteer who thinks that staff positions are not needed or who wants to rush in and take over. When the axe falls, concerned volunteers may try to make the best of a bad situation. Concerned and thinking volunteers will make a conscious choice about whether to work at a formerly staff task or channel their energies into advocacy and policy development which will lead to the re-establishment of sufficient funding for necessary positions. Both kinds of volunteers are needed. Over the long haul, they will probably help create as many or more positions as have been lost.

Given the uncertainties of the present, it is easier to be optimistic about the long run than to assure the job security of today's staff. Nonetheless, there is little to be gained from allowing or encouraging paid personnel to force their operational volunteer co-workers to express their commitment to The Cause by allying themselves with the cause of preserving a specific staff position. There is even less to be gained by treating volunteers like illegal aliens. Both staff and operational volunteers are caught in larger issues which will not be resolved by pettiness at this level, however understandable its source.

Another instance when operations volunteers may be accused of supplanting staff is a strike situation. To scab or not to scab is the volunteer's choice from labor's point of view; to keep things going on the "We'll show 'em" principle the choice from management's point of view. Both sides will claim to be the most concerned about client welfare, leaving the operations volunteer in a no-win situation. The best advice for ALL volunteers is: Do not get caught off guard! Strikes, like other crises, do not hatch overnight; some people somewhere are making contingency plans for if and how to keep services going. If they are not talking to each other and/or including volunteers in this facet of the process, volunteers should demand information on which to base their personal decisions about what they will do. A hospital strike may have different ramifications for appropriate volunteer action than a school strike, for example. Individuals and organizations also have ample advocacy opportunities before and during the crisis. They may seek ways to get all points of view aired and dealt with fairly and may try to keep some communications open so that the long-range goals of the service being threatened are harmed as little as possible during the short-run disruption.

The one thing labor and management may agree on is that the dispute is just between them and everyone else should stay out of it. This writer believes that is nonsense. The human services establishment is hanging by a thread as it is. Its present and future hinge on increasing the public's philosophical support and financial commitment (taxed or donated) in a way which is substantively different from private industry. Neither "side" can afford to assume that they are the only parties with something at stake. Volunteers who have already demonstrated their commitment to the particular area of concern have the right and obligation to be kept informed and involved if their concerns relate to the larger, longer-range aspects of the dispute or to what happens to clients during the disruption.

This does not mean that volunteers should mediate or dictate, only that they should be acknowledged as interested parties for certain sections of the debate. Any involvement and intervention by volunteers is a delicate matter and should not be undertaken if the volunteers have decided to "take sides" between labor and management and hope to become a "fifth column" by getting information from inside the enemy camp. If the volunteers want to be trusted, they will have to conduct themselves with honesty and discretion.

Given an understanding of the many faces of operational volunteering and in light of the complex issues generated in staff/volunteer relationships, the traditional "supplement not supplant" catch phrase may have outlived its usefulness. It clarifies little and seems to be valuable only as a sop to professionally insecure staff or as a put-down of undisciplined volunteers.

7.2c The Recruitment Illusion

Hope springs eternal in the heart of volunteerism. The studies which show that a substantial minority of Americans volunteer leave us with the information that a substantial majority do not. What an incredible, almost limitless pool of potentially willing souls to be recruited if only we can be creative enough! On bad days it might even be fun to fantasize about the day when we have waiting lists of potential volunteers. It is certainly a possibility and an admirable goal to increase the percentage of the population which volunteers. Certainly the optimism this information engenders should not be snatched from those staff and volunteers who are responsible for recruiting. However, it creates problems in the existing relationships between operations volunteers and the organizations in which they work.

The big one is inadequate planning and goal setting at the policy and administrative levels. It is not hard to be "realistic" about how much staff one can hire at a given time, and considerable thought is given to defining and prioritizing those jobs. But when money and staff run out, it is tempting to conclude that volunteers can fill in the gaps and to leap immediately into a vigorous recruitment campaign without giving enough attention to what the recruits will be doing and what the organization will do if the recruitment effort falls short. (This assumption is also used in organizations with no paid personnel.) But is more necessarily better? Is there such a thing as too many? Will we discontinue a program if x number of volunteers is not recruited? Is a warm body better than no body at all? How far can we lower any defined qualifications in order to fill the slot before we jeopardize what we are trying to do? These questions are often unasked and therefore unanswered.

When the illusion that recruitment is our only problem is shattered and we are left shorthanded, we are more likely to extract a "little extra" from the current pool of volunteers (and those staff who are not eligible for overtime pay) than to reassess and realign service goals. Policy volunteers in some organizations "pitch in" rather than stick to their task of making hard decisions. The "little extra" often becomes a lot more and exploits those who are already committed. It can create a siege mentality which makes those already recruited resent those who said no, thus creating a wall which may hamper future recruitment efforts. It may also force the good guys to wonder if they are masochistic rather than altruistic.

The gap between potential and actual numbers of volunteers should and often does generate a strong sense of appreciation for the volunteers who are at work. Yet even appreciation can be carried to unhealthy extremes. So scarce and precious are the enlisted, warm bodies that, whatever their limitations, many organizations go out of their way to keep them happy at all costs. Sometimes the cost is tolerating poor performance, failing to make demands on volunteers which will enhance organizational goals and oddly the volunteers' satisfaction, and otherwise walking on eggs around The Volunteer. This may delay but will not prevent everyone's getting frustrated at some point. The volunteer is not the client or the cause, and recruitment is not the first step in improving the effectiveness of operations volunteering.

7.2d Burned Up, Burned Out, or Simply Unreliable

In many circles volunteers are notorious for voting with their feet, for "firing" organizations and for being unreliable. Certainly in any group of human beings as diverse as volunteers, it is inevitable that some portion can only be called unreliable. However, some of the behavior exhibited by volunteers which gets called unreliability is actually a misfit between organizational and individual needs. It is important for volunteers and organizations to examine these other possibilities before writing each other off in a fit of pique.

It should be clear by now that there is ample opportunity for a misfit to occur. Examples from our discussion thus far include:

A direct service or advocacy volunteer in a housekeeping slot.
Vice versa.
An operations volunteer in a policy position.
Vice versa.
An anti-deadline person in a fundraising campaign.
Any volunteer with an ill-defined job.
Being a scapegoat for all inadequacies in the organization.
Being taken for granted.
Being denied access to certain options due to age and sex bias.
Wearing too many hats within one organization.
Wearing too many hats for more than one.
Some warrant further discussion.

1) Open-ended Commitments. Much operations volunteering involves tasks which even if they are defined as a few hours a week go on year-round and/or indefinitely into the future. Unlike policy volunteering where some concept of term is usually built in, operations volunteers are recruited with the hope (on the part of the recruiter) that these people will stick around for a long time. Often there is no mutually defined review point which would give both individual and organization a face-saving way out. Since the assignments are very part-time, few worry about whether or not the volunteer is getting bored, stale, or tired. After all, what is the difference for a few hours a week?

2) Lack of new opportunities for personal growth. Personal growth is often interpreted to mean advancement. Within the operations chain advancement may be an appropriate concept in situations where, for example, a particularly skilled and sensitive direct service or advocacy volunteer would make a good trainer, recruiter, or other support volunteer. The change of pace might well be a tribute to the person's accomplishments.

Some notions of personal growth as advancement can lead to problems. Rewarding a loyal operations volunteer with a policy position may work, but only if the volunteer is interested in and qualified for it. Sometimes a volunteer is "rewarded" by being hired for a paid position. That this is even perceived as advancement speaks of our obsession that a paid job is always higher ranking than a volunteer one. Depending on the volunteer and the job, this transition might offer personal growth and be appropriate for the organization. However, the volunteer should not expect special consideration or automatic hiring if the organization has a better applicant, feels that fresh blood is needed, or does not wish to set that precedent.

A particularly tricky variation on this theme is hiring a former policy volunteer, particularly a board member, usually in some subordinate staff capacity. The shift from forest management to tree tending with the concomitant change in information access and level of decision making may be hard for the new jobholder to accept. It may be equally difficult for other staff and volunteers to shift gears in their relationships with this individual. Again it is not impossible, but it should not be undertaken casually.

3) Competing Commitments. People who volunteer are apt to do so for more than one organization. They will give priority to those tasks which are most urgent and satisfying. One organization's loss may well be another's gain. Even a volunteer who is skilled at not getting overextended will get caught in overlapping commitments, i.e., between finishing one task and starting another.

There may also be changes in a volunteer's personal situation at home or at work which will "compete" for time and energy previously devoted to the organization. One young rising corporate star of this writer's acquaintance resigned from most of the numerous policy positions he held in several volunteer organizations. His reason was that he wanted to be a troop leader for his son's Boy Scout experience. He realized that this opportunity would come only once and that he could resume policy tasks at a later point. If that was unreliability, we probably need more of it.

When all of the ambiguity and ambivalence which is reflected in our treatment of volunteers catches up with individual volunteers, they generally react in one of two ways. Some get burned up and walk away from a task or an organization. Occasionally they swear off volunteering altogether, i.e., behave in an "unreliable" way. Others burn out. They simply get tired and may not know when to quit. As their performance slips, they not only frustrate themselves but they also unwittingly feed the notion that you cannot count on or expect much from volunteers. Burn-up is dramatic and probably healthier for the individual. Burnout is insidious and creeps up on the volunteer. Both threaten the organization.

In becoming burned up or burned out, volunteers are no different from staff or people in general for that matter. Why should it surprise us so when it happens to a volunteer? Before bandying the word unreliable around, organizations need to take a hard and honest look at all the facts in individual cases and in the aggregate. It is quite possible that their own approach to the use of volunteers is creating or at least abetting the problems we have so glibly called unreliability and so insensitively dumped on all volunteers.

7.3 INTRODUCING THE "UNPAID" STAFF

Now that we have looked at the types of operations volunteering and at some potential flaws in working with and as these volunteers, we can begin to build a better framework for improving effectiveness. Before getting too specific about activities which lead in this direction, it is important to make sure that the conceptual base for that framework is mutually understood.

We have made a distinction between policy and operations which makes sense almost intuitively for those who give it any thought, even if these are not the terms customarily used in a particular organization. Each chain has a distinct function in the organization which must be appreciated and worked with on its own terms. However, we have given lip service to the distinction in ways which unwittingly confuse rather than clarify it.

One of these is to view policy development as decision making and operations as doing. This glosses over a fact which is no doubt painfully clear by now: Decision making does not end when a board meeting adjourns. The translation of generalized policies and program goals into meaningful activities involves decision making at all levels of the operations chain as well as the policy chain.

Another way we have distinguished policy and operations is to capsulize it as volunteer/staff or board/staff. Volunteers make policy; staff implement it. Ah, if it were only that simple! We have already seen that effective policy making involves constructive interplay between the abstract and the specific, between forest managers and tree tenders. Attempts to disassociate one from the other for the sake of convenience and presumed clarity are artificial even in the policy chain of organizations with staff.

When it comes to operations, the distinction can also be misleading. For example, emphasis on volunteer/staff terminology encourages organizations which do not have staff to ignore the discreteness between policy and operations and to forget to expect their members to change hats. It also ignores volunteers in public agencies where there is no volunteer board structure. In organizations with both volunteer boards and paid staff it has the effect of leaving out the large numbers of volunteers who are not in the policy chain. Or rather it leaves them floundering in a large grey area without a real niche in the organization's chains of accountability.

Though the volunteer/staff dichotomy does not accurately define the difference between policy and operations, there is one way in which the customary terminology can be valuable. In a very real sense, operations volunteers are staff. They are "on duty" to help implement the policies and program goals defined by the policy makers. Presumably they are performing tasks which someone has determined to be necessary and appropriate, has defined into work units, and has assigned to interested and qualified persons. In effective organizations this is more than a presumption; it is a fact. Operations volunteers are viewed as an integral part of the personnel resources available to the organization. It is understood that any hiring decision requires a fit between individual qualifications and organizational needs and represents a mutual, potentially long-term investment by hirer and hiree in order to assure productive performance.

Operational decision making, i.e., how to distribute and accomplish certain tasks is often done in groups such as staff or committee meetings and hence requires teamwork and a clear division of labor. Operations personnel whether paid or volunteer are more likely than policy volunteers to have discrete, individual tasks which can be performed and evaluated on their own merits as well as on their contribution to the total accomplishment of the organization. Corporateness, as it was described in Chapter 6, is not a factor with operations personnel; division of labor and formalized accountability are germane.

In other words, it is in the realm of operations volunteering that our view of volunteering as work and not play offers exciting possibilities for improving present practice. A concept of these volunteers as staff invites greater intentionality in the selection, placement and supervision of operations volunteers. No one would dream of hiring everyone who walks in the door asking for a paid job and then turning them loose at any task they choose without further direction. On the other hand, many job descriptions and job requirements are not so rigid as to require programmed robots and to preclude some accomodation to the special interests, skills, needs and idiosyncracies of the jobholder while still addressing organizational needs.

On a very tangible level, this may include adjustment of work hours as well as provisions for personal time, sick time and vacation. At another level it means utilizing fully those unique talents of the jobholder which pertain to organizational goals, promoting employee development, and strengthening performance as necessary in those areas which are not the employee's forte through ongoing training and supervision. It means establishing and maintaining a working relationship as long as it is mutually acceptable, assuming that at the bottom line the employer is primarily concerned with protecting "company" interests and the employees their personal interests. It also suggests that maintaining such relationships will have some downs as well as ups and allows for appeals, grievances, severance and resignation procedures which help assure that termination of the working relationship is not treated in a cavalier fashion by either party. Organizations with sound policies and procedures for employed personnel will find many of the same principles applicable to the use of operations volunteers. Organizations with employed staff but without workable personnel policies have problems beyond the scope of a book on volunteering. All groups would benefit from a personnel management approach to operations volunteers.

It is widely assumed that the major drawback of this approach to working with volunteers is that if the working relationship is not accompanied by a paycheck the employer has no right to demand satisfactory performance and has no control over the employees. Put more gently, this fallacy assumes that mutual accountability is out of the question. Certainly if the paycheck in question constitutes the worker's livelihood, he or she will think extra hard before jeopardizing a given working situation and may put up with more foolishness and abuse than a volunteer. From the employer's viewpoint, firing a paid employee is not the simple matter it once was, and at least in the legal sense it may be easier to get rid of an unsatisfactory volunteer.

This dollars-and-cents concept is too simplistic an approach to motivation and accountability for both paid and unpaid personnel. For one thing it assumes that the paycheck itself is the only item of concern among employed personnel. The libraries are full of material showing that workers expect more from their jobs than money. They want appreciation for the work done, a sense of having done something useful, growth opportunities and the right to participate in some of the decision making surrounding their work as well as good wages and job security. The "human resources management" and "future of the workplace" literature offers considerable insight into contemporary worker expectations, most of which is as germane to volunteers as it is to employed personnel.

Secondly, this dollars-and-cents view of accountability obscures the fact that volunteers are not in reality giving their services free of charge. Thanks to the efforts of the "professional volunteer" advocates, we are beginning to remove the stigma from admitting that volunteers are doing selfless acts for some selfish reasons. If they have a need to feel useful and/or appreciated, they expect payback in these terms. If they can do good and at the same time make new business contacts or advance their career skills, this is not automatically a contaminant.

A provocative and more productive way of looking at volunteers' motivation and "pay" is to think of volunteer work as an exchange relationship rather than a gift relationship. Larry Bohleber adapted sociologist George Homan's social exchange theory to apply to volunteers in this way:[5]

Volunteers are volunteering as a means toward desired goals.
All volunteer activities cost the volunteer something.
Volunteers "economize," i.e., keep costs below rewards.
Only economical activities tend to be perpetuated.

This could mean that the volunteer whose sole motivation is to repay a favor owed to a friend would spend a few hours stuffing envelopes once but would not want to be called on time after time. Or if a particular volunteer job requires full use of known skills, offers growth potential and personal recognition, and appeals philosophically, the volunteer may invest considerable time, energy and money in a Herculean task.

The exchange concept applies equally to the organization using volunteers where the premises could read:

> Organizations use volunteers as a means of moving toward desired goals.
> All volunteer activities cost the organization something.
> Organizations "economize."
> Only economical activities tend to be perpetuated.

For the organization this may mean weighing the investment of the staff time required to cultivate volunteers against the value of the work performed and the good will generated by the satisfied volunteer.

Caution: The exchange approach with its emphasis on economy may be useful in helping to do a more realistic and balanced "cost analysis" of volunteering. (We have focused thus far on the dynamics; dollar costs will be examined in Chapter 8.) However, beware of simplistic false economies. For example, paid staff may believe that by definition volunteers are uneconomical, and volunteers may believe their contribution is priceless. Both could use the exchange theory to rationalize unrealistic demands, and we would then be in the same bind in which we started.

If we accept the idea that operations volunteers are in reality "paid" staff, though not paid in dollars, we can approach hiring and placement of them as a negotiation of price. Once the price is mutually agreed to and fully understood, the nonaccountability ploy loses its punch, and we can move on to being more creative about strengthening everyone's understanding and use of accountability as a positive force.

7.4 STRENGTHENING THE OPERATIONS CHAIN

Many of the issues addressed thus far carry the seeds of their own resolution. If the conceptual framework we have developed is used in conjunction with the very fine how-to materials which are already available and which are designed to serve specific substantive areas, we will be well along the road to greater effectiveness. As an ending point for this chapter and, more importantly, as a starting point for taking action, we can summarize the requisites for strengthening the operations chain under four basic headings.

7.4a Getting the Organizational Act Together

By this is meant that most organizations have a ways to go in defining goals and objectives and in refining their total structure. The sloppiness and fogginess which have characterized much of our handling of operations volunteers are as much symptom as cause of these more basic problems. The solutions must begin at the top levels of policy making and administration. Specific activities at this level pertaining to the use of operations volunteers include:

--Review all personnel resources, those available now and those needed.

--Develop job definitions and job descriptions which relate to organizational objectives, i.e., define expected results.

--Develop and use personnel policies and procedures for volunteers as well as for paid-in-dollars staff.

--Use contracts with volunteers which describe what is expected and what the conditions of "employment" are. Build in some definition of term so that the volunteer is not taking on a lifetime commitment. If there is training required and/or a minimum period which the organization expects from the volunteer, say so up front.

--Know who is accountable to whom for what. Delegate management responsibilities accordingly. E.g., an organizational maintenance volunteer who helps the paid public relations staff make and distribute posters should be accountable to and supervised by that person. Both of them are accountable to the executive director who is in turn ultimately responsible to the board. A teacher's aide is not accountable to the PTA, even if the same person is active in the PTA and may have heard about the aide position at its meeting. VOLUNTEERS NEED NOT ALWAYS BE ACCOUNTABLE TO OTHER VOLUNTEERS.

7.4b Building Adequate Support Systems

At a more intermediate level, organizations which rely on volunteers should assure the development of structures and procedures which will translate the general policies into workable systems. For the operations volunteers, this may mean having relevant training, having supervisory conferences and consultations with someone who can give them perspective, and being sent to appropriate conferences and community events which expand skills and horizons. For staff it may mean providing assistance in planning work assignments for volunteers and receiving training in personnel management. Recognition events for volunteers and staff appreciation functions are important support components.

The key here is that responsibility for support should be defined and assigned so that adequate time for recruitment, training, supervision, and morale boosting is created rather than assumed. In all but the smallest organizations, there is a role for an operations volunteer co-ordinator. Large agencies and institutions are beginning to hire people to do these tasks; other organizations such as the Boy and Girl Scouts have structures in which the support function is shared by staff and volunteers. In many groups the responsibility is just sort of dumped on the president and committee chairs.

In no organization will the establishment of a co-ordinating position or structure magically resolve all the problems we have discussed. Nor will it absolve policy makers, administrators and individual staff and volunteers from their responsibilities to perform effectively. It can, however, greatly reduce friction and facilitate both getting the work done and improving internal working relationships.

7.4c Practicing Assertive Etiquette

While we are getting the organization's act together and developing adequate support systems—and beyond that time, actually, we can improve working relationships by being more thoughtful of co-workers, staff and volunteers. While we are thrashing out our new definitions and working arrangements, we have choices other than getting burned up and burned out or being hostile and suspicious. We can simply be more polite and more aware of the impact of some of our actions. For example, it is rude for a staff person who is expecting a volunteer to say, "Oh, hi," with a note of surprise while scraping off a corner of the desk to make room for said volunteer. It is thoughtless of a volunteer to drift in unannounced and interrupt a busy staff person. It is inconsiderate for anyone to call up at the last minute and expect a volunteer to drop everything and pitch in when the request for help could have been made three weeks ago. It is insensitive as well as shortsighted for an organization not to provide opportunities for all levels of personnel to have some sort of say about what is going on and to have channels for venting discontents and grievances.

Individuals, whether volunteer or staff, and organizations have their limits and have the right to acknowledge them openly and without guilt. However, we can say no or acknowledge there are problems without trouncing on each other's egos. We can treat co-workers as people with dignity without getting mushy about it, and we can behave professionally without getting crisp and prickly. Since operations volunteers and the organizations in which they work are presumably in the people-serving business, civility should start at home.

7.4d Hanging In There

As the doctor reportedly says to overweight patients, "You did not get into this state overnight, and you will not get out of it that way either." Improving the effectiveness of operations volunteering requires changing long-established attitudes and behaviors, a process which will be facilitated by both assertive discontent and gentle persuasion. Crash diets and overnight organizational restructuring will probably not produce the miracles we would like. The organization which uses operational volunteers can only be fair to itself and to its personnel if it understands the long- and short-term implications of operations volunteering.

References

[1] Examples of this feminist position can be found in:

Doris B. Gold, "Women and Voluntarism," WOMAN IN SEXIST SOCIETY: STUDIES IN POWER AND POWERLESSNESS, ed. Vivian Gornick and Barbara K. Moran (New York: Basic Books, Inc., 1971) pp. 384-400.

Francine D. Blau, "Comment on Mueller's 'Economic Determinants of Volunteer Work by Women'," SIGNS: JOURNAL OF WOMEN AND CULTURE IN SOCIETY, Vol. 2, No. 1, Autumn, 1976, pp. 253 ff.

[2] Herta Loeser and Janet Falon, "Women Board Members and Volunteer Agencies," FOUNDATION NEWS, September/ October 1977, pp. 27-31.

[3] Sara Evans, PERSONAL POLITICS: THE ROOTS OF WOMEN'S LIBERATION IN THE CIVIL RIGHTS MOVEMENT AND THE NEW LEFT (New York: Alfred A. Knopf, 1979).

[4] Eleanore Carruth, "Some Executives' Wives Are Executives too," FORTUNE, December, 1973, pp. 114-119.

[5] Larry W. Bohleber, "The Exchange Theory," VOLUNTARY ACTION LEADERSHIP, Summer, 1979, pp. 16-17.

8

ACKNOWLEDGING THE VOLUNTEERS

8.1 THE TWO-WAY STREET

In Chapters 6 and 7 we examined some of the
structures, functions, and dynamics which influence the
roles and performance of volunteers within existing
organizations. We looked at components which can be
applied within organizations to clarify volunteer roles
and to strengthen the volunteers' sense of accountability. Both of these should lead to a more workable,
productive relationship between volunteers and the
organizations where they are at work. Indeed, the
degree to which these are understood, respected, and
dealt with will be the major factor in determining
whether or not volunteers will be used effectively.

There are, however, issues which exceed the capacity of any one organization or any one set of volunteers to resolve by unilateral and internal efforts exclusively. These have to do with where and how much to augment the attention and support given to volunteers and volunteerism by society at large. If we believe that volunteers are doing useful and necessary work and if we are going to enhance their performance by requiring greater accountability of them, it is appropriate and, in fact, imperative that society reciprocate not with pious platitudes but with substantive institutionalized recognition of their importance.

The topics included in this chapter will range from the immediately useful to the remotely relevant, though which ones fall in which category will vary with the reader's point of view. The premise for incorporating them under the same heading is that they all represent points where fairer and more equitable recognition can be given to the volunteers' contribution to society. On most of them action will be required in more than one arena, but the cumulative effect of all such activity will be more positive for volunteerism if the activity is placed in context: Accountability is a two-way street.

8.2 PAYING TO DO GOOD

Perhaps we have inflation and the energy crisis to thank for bringing out of the closet a very delicate issue: money. There is usually at least a minimal expense associated with volunteer jobs. Doing volunteer work can get quite expensive for the volunteer. This means that volunteers are not really working for free; they are paying for the privilege of doing good.

As long as Lady Bountiful dominated our image of volunteers, it was easy to rationalize that she could afford to pay for her own transportation, meals, childcare, etc. Furthermore if we needed extra money and had to pass the hat or ask for endless bakesale donations, so what? She could afford tnese sporadic little extras. This casual disregard of costs is an important and tangible reason why the group of citizens most likely to be found volunteering are middle-aged and middle-class or above. An insidious side effect has been to discourage the less affluent from volunteering not only because they truly could not afford it but also because they have not wished to add embarrassment to their already uncomfortable lack of discretionary income. No one likes putting himself in a situation which might require admitting that he cannot keep up with the Bountifuls.

What a good solid economic pinch does is to democratize the problem and to make it real to a wider cross section of the community. For example, as the price of gasoline skyrocketed, rich and poor alike began to think twice about where they needed to go and why. When there were actual shortages and gasoline was not available at any price, individuals and organizations were forced to re-evaluate the ways they scheduled activities or meetings. Some changes in practice resulted, not the least of which was a change in attitude whereby one is now less likely to be considered tacky if forced to say that something is getting too expensive.

While an individual can choose to volunteer or not for any reason including financial limits, organizations which rely on volunteers need to give careful attention to the dollar costs to volunteers and the organization for the work being performed. They must understand that the costs to the volunteer may create a financial barrier to an otherwise qualified person. The organization can then define what its responsibility should and will be for offsetting those costs, and the results of this decision reflected in the operating budget.

We have already discussed the case for viewing volunteers as an integral part of the organization. If we also recognize that being affluent is not a prerequisite for doing most volunteer jobs effectively, it follows that one way to broaden the recruitment base is to lower financial barriers. If these statements are true, the first volunteer related item in the ideal budget will be reimbursement of out-of-pocket expenses:

--transportation (bus fare, mileage), parking and tolls related to services rendered

　　　　--meals REQUIRED as part of a volunteer job (such
　　　　as a Board president representing the organiza-
　　　　tion at a United Way annual meeting)
　　　　--toll and long-distance telephone charges
　　　　--postage, copying, supplies
　　　　--childcare while performing volunteer service

All of these involve cash outlays which the volunteers
would not incur if they opted to stay at home or at
work. Reimbursement would free them from having to rule
out an expenditure of time which they could afford
because the concomitant expenditure of money is out of
reach. Since volunteering is work and not play, the
organization can justify reimbursement in principle as a
cost of doing business.

Optional items to be considered for reimbursement
are meals which occur because a mealtime works best for
getting people together for a meeting or which are
indicated when an operational task extends over a long
period of time on any one day. Certainly everyone has
to eat. However, if the meals are taken in a restaurant, catered, or brought in from the corner delicates-
sen, they may cost more money than the volunteer can or
would like to spend. Building the meal payment into the
unwritten job description may raise a barrier. This
item is presented as optional even in the ideal case
because there are viable alternatives for the organization short of picking up the tab: Schedule meetings or
activities at other times. If a mealtime is essential,
consider a location and a format which give volunteers
the choice of buying the meal offered, "brown-bagging"
it, or not eating then at all. Then make sure the
atmosphere is such that they do not feel compelled to
explain why they made which choice.

Uniforms are another out-of-pocket expense incurred
by volunteers in some settings. If a uniform is
absolutely required, every effort should be made to
ensure that volunteers do not have to pay for
them. However, reimbursement per se is not the only
alternative and may not be the best one. Uniform
supplies represent a longer-term investment by the
organization than may be justified by the volunteers'
tenure in their jobs, and there are other ways of
addressing these expenses. For example, if the

"uniform" is a T-shirt for a coach, the cost of the coach's shirt can be covered by fees team members pay. If the volunteer work is done at a central location such as a hospital, the organization can operate a "uniform cupboard," assigning uniforms as needed and establishing controls so that volunteers are aware of their responsibility to take care of the items borrowed.

In some cases a uniform is not required but is highly recommended, and/or the volunteer work is not performed in a central setting where the organization can keep control over uniform distribution. In these instances a uniform exchange or uniform rental system may suffice, as long as the organization is sincere in its statements that the uniforms are desirable but optional. In no instance should the organization take the position that the volunteers have to wear something and it might as well be the official uniform. This can lead to sloppiness in interpreting why the uniform is important to the program and to insensitivity about the barriers created by the cost of a uniform.

Though at risk of sounding frothy, it seems appropriate to mention here that another money-related problem can be "proper" attire. Except where we are talking about uniforms, clothing cannot be considered a reimbursable expense. However, like the cost of meals, it can be an insidious barrier to volunteer involvement. This is more appropriately treated as an issue of sensitivity than of direct expense. For example, a well-intentioned staff person of this writer's acquaintance once told a newly-recruited, low-income board member to be sure to wear stockings to the meetings. "What did she think I would wear?" was the angry, hurt response from one who fortunately cooled down and went on to serve long and well. What it boils down to is this: If it is important to have an economic cross section of volunteers involved, do not conduct business in the most expensive restaurant in town where anything less than a three-piece business suit or a mink stole is considered gauche. Sometimes it is the little things that count.

The issue of stipends is another question which arises in discussions about the costs of volunteering and how to deal with them. By stipend we usually mean a token amount per hour or activity paid to volunteers in lieu of reimbursing actual expenses and/or as a little extra enticement in recruiting and/or as a gesture of appreciation. Token usually means less than the prevailing wages and less than the minimum wage. However, this writer believes that such payments further muddy the already cloudy waters surrounding staff/volunteer relations and may divert attention and money from getting staff salaries up to some sort of morally acceptable and competitive level. Payment of stipends may have longer-term diluting effects on the unique contributions volunteering makes to our society precisely because the volunteers are not making their living at this work. The implications of this will be discussed in greater detail in Chapter 9. For our purposes here, it suffices to say that, for community-based volunteering, stipends are inappropriate. If the volunteer is living away from home as in the Peace Corps or VISTA, the "stipend" may be necessary to cover living expenses but should be viewed as such.

The rationale for reimbursement is perhaps easier to develop than the mechanics. Reimbursement requires a kind of recordkeeping by the individual and the organization which has not been customary in volunteering. When added to the existing paperwork demands faced by an organization, it may seem like the last straw. Many volunteers are not in the habit of keeping formal accounts of the time and money they spend in volunteer work, and they are annoyed by this bureaucratic intrusion on their spontaneous good works.

Caught in the notion that true volunteers should be free help, some volunteers are uncomfortable with accepting money even if it is only an attempt to keep volunteer work a wash item in their personal budgets. The most common reaction, particularly from those of moderate income or better, is that the organization's money should be spent on "service" and not on them. This unquestionably shows genuine commitment on their part, but it also reflects a false modesty about the volunteers' contribution to the services provided and a lack of awareness of the impact of nonreimbursement on the less affluent.

Old habits and attitudes are hard to break. When reimbursement is launched, it must be carefully and positively promoted as the step forward which it is. A good reimbursement program would have the following elements:

--A clear policy statement covering all volunteers and defining which expenses will be reimbursed, at what rate and at what intervals. (e.g., monthly or quarterly checks; out of petty cash with proper receipts)

--An expense account record for each volunteer

--Assignment of recordkeeping responsibilities to one specific person in the organization

--A step-by-step written outline which describes the entire process and which is carefully explained to all volunteers and to pertinent staff.

Common sense suggests that, even if the money were budgeted and available, some persons are able to absorb their volunteer expenses and, because of their commitment, are willing to do so. In these cases it may be foolishness bordering on wastefulness to force reimbursement on them and to add the necessary paperwork to the burden of another volunteer or a staff person. Nonetheless, it is important to separate contributions of money from contributions of time. People who have both to share may either return the reimbursement as a gift by means of a separate transaction or be given a place on the expense forms to indicate that they do not wish to be reimbursed. It is equally important, though, that all volunteers keep and submit expense records if a reimbursement policy is to be effective. These records are needed to provide data which the organization can use in making more realistic budget projections in the event the proportion of reimbursed/nonreimbursed volunteers changes. Also those volunteers who need reimbursement must not be made to feel different and somehow less valuable to the organization.

Common sense also suggests that, since sufficient funds are rarely available, a reimbursement program may have to be limited to very specific items and be available only if requested. This is certainly better than nothing but requires sensitive, discreet handling by the person responsible for monitoring it. The rules of thumb for organizations offering reimbursement are to be equitable and to be prepared to pay for what you have said you will. Nothing is more self-defeating for the organization and awkward for the individual than a stance which conveys the mixed message that we have budgeted for this reimbursement but we surely hope you do not ask for it.

8.3 OPTIONAL AT EXTRA COST

Some expenses are not regularly incurred by volunteers in the course of performing their duties, but they do involve costs which should be incorporated into organization budgets rather than taken out of the volunteers' pockets: orientation and training for new volunteers, in-service education programs for continuing ones, recognition events for all volunteers, and conferences/conventions for selected representatives, volunteer or staff. These items are somewhat better established as legitimate expenses than the out-of-pocket routine costs just discussed, and they are generally quite palatable because they seem more manageable. However, experience indicates that we have a way to go in seeing that they are provided for adequately because more manageable usually means either dispensable or the province of those able to pay.

Rarely do organizations require volunteers to pay for their orientation and training, though this writer recently saw an ad for volunteers which said, "Sign up now; 15-hour training and $10 for materials." They are more likely to scrimp on materials, refreshments, and/or planning time. Yet all of these constitute an investment which would get the volunteers off to a more informed and enthusiastic start and which may well pay dividends exponentially in terms of long-run volunteer effectiveness. In-service or other continuing education opportunities within the organization can be equally useful but are offered even less frequently than initial training as much because we do not think about them as because we cannot afford them.

Recognition is often viewed as a choice between a simple thank you and an elaborate banquet, with the former seeming more reasonable. Thank yous are important, but so is formal recognition. There are many appropriate and inexpensive alternatives. One school volunteer program, for example, gives athletic passes to those volunteers who work thirty or more hours per semester. One list proposed "101 Ways" to offer volunteer recognition. On this score too, we are usually limited more by lack of imagination than lack of money.

Outside educational programs, conferences and conventions present trickier problems. They have in common the aura of "junket" when in reality they are opportunities for some very intense, demanding work. If the function is out of town and if a city tour or gala banquet is part of the package, that does not necessarily constitute an all-expenses-paid vacation for the organization's representatives. All of these types of functions can add immeasurably to the individual delegates' organization-related skills, their understanding of larger concerns, their enthusiasm for The Cause, and their commitment to the organization. It is important to consider key volunteers as well as key staff for such growth opportunities, and it is appropriate to expect that these individuals "repay" the organization by making a commitment of longevity and service to allow time for debriefing, feedback and incorporating new ideas into organizational operation. Since a post-conference commitment is not generally "enforceable," the control over repayment lies in careful prior selection of representatives. The main point is that if a person is asked to be a delegate, the organization should be prepared to cover expenses. If, on the other hand, the individual asks to attend, the organization can decide what it has to gain by helping defray the costs, and any "terms" for sharing them can be considered negotiable.

One obstacle to adequate budgeting for these events is lack of timely information. Organizations are barraged almost daily with flyers about exciting, upcoming conferences and training events. It is annoying to learn dates and costs too late in a budgeting process to make proper allowance for them. It

160

can be very frustrating to have sent representatives to a program early in the fiscal year and then to find that later programs would have been higher priority but the money is all gone. "First come, first served" may work from the point of view of event sponsors, but it prevents effective organizational decision making. Perhaps presidents and executives should make it a point to inform sponsors as to why they could not send participants. In the meantime, organizations should do the best they can to provide appropriate opportunities to appropriate personnel and to minimize the costs to those asked to participate.

This obstacle should never arise in relation to conventions, for, in addition to individual skill- and morale-building functions, conventions are business meetings which affect the organization and to which it is entitled and expected to send delegates. The frequency with which they are held is mandated by constitution. Because of the exigencies of convention planning particularly at the national level, dates and locations are apt to be determined and known well in advance. Obviously if an organization is located in Maine and the next national convention is in Hawaii (or vice versa), the problem is of a different magnitude than that of attending regional or state meetings. Nevertheless, full convention participation, i.e., sending the maximum number of voting delegates, should be an organizational objective, and proper budgeting and fundraising done to assure that delegate selection is not based solely on who can pay for the airplane ticket.

Both routine and special expenses do affect individual volunteers, and organizations need to explore and handle the dollar issues. This discussion might just as well have gone into the last two chapters on how organizations can promote volunteer effectiveness except for two factors. First, there is a tendency within and among organizations to treat all of these items as optional or unaffordable, an inclination reinforced by attitudes among donors, taxpayers and funding sources. As a result, these budget items are often the last included and the first excluded. In the short run utilities, supplies and staff salaries win hands down every time. Yet over the long haul an investment in the volunteers will have a substantial positive impact on organization effectiveness as well as on the usefulness and satisfaction of individual volunteers.

Secondly, there is some concern that organizations will use reimbursement to give themselves a competitive edge in volunteer recruitment and that we will lose something valuable if volunteers start to select their assignments on the basis of getting a better deal. Thus a persistent and consistent effort by all organizations which use volunteers to budget adequately for all these types of expenses would contribute to greater effectiveness in volunteering by:

--eliminating some of the barriers to volunteering by some groups of citizens and freeing all to choose those concerns which are most urgent to them,

--formalizing our commitment to making it possible for volunteers to separate cash commitments from service ones,

--reducing the chance that the money difference results in cutthroat or unfair competition among organizations, and, most importantly,

--reinforcing the notion that volunteers are already involved at levels of service above nonvolunteer citizens, that they are performing essential work which would otherwise have to be paid for or left undone, and that we cannot afford NOT to help them break even financially.

One last thought: There may be volunteer groups which are sufficiently homogeneous or in which all members bear costs fairly equitably where attempts to reimburse particularly the routine expenses would be absurd. There are few organizations financially capable of covering these expenses adequately even if they want to. Regardless of which factors may prevail, it is useful for all volunteer organizations to go through the exercise of evaluating volunteer expenditures so that they may at least be more sensitive to the dollar implications of the demands they are making on the volunteers. For example, if you had to reimburse for mileage, would it be worth asking someone to spend $1.00 on gasoline searching the town for a 50¢ markoff on supplies? Would it make sense to arrange a needed one-to-one conference around an already scheduled meeting rather than to require two trips? In other words, no long-term purpose is served by nickel-and-diming people to death. If being sensitive is the most we can do, it is surely also the least we can do.

8.4   THE RISKS OF DOING GOOD

Just as volunteers run up expenses which they could have avoided by watching television instead, they may also run extra financial risk by virtue of being involved. We live in a very litigious age where every slip-up or alleged slip-up seems to become the subject of a lawsuit and often involves staggering sums of money for legal fees, settlements, and damages before the matter is closed. While in actuality volunteers are not often sued, it only takes one news story about a youth leader being accused of gross negligence in a tragic accident or one report of a hospital or school board being charged with mismanagement to make all volunteers and the organizations they serve extremely apprehensive about when the axe will fall on them. In fact, we cannot know and thus are right to be concerned. There are several different kinds of insurance which organizations can consider for the protection of individual volunteers as well as for corporate peace of mind.

Of special, though not exclusive, relevance to operations volunteers, for example, are such coverages as:

Accident--covering accidents occurring during normal organizational activities by participants and volunteers. May be additional coverage and become effective after individual's other policies have been exceeded.

Public Liability--protecting volunteers (possibly in the same policy as staff) in suits which might arise against them in their performance of work for the organization.

163

Nonownership Automobile Liability--providing additional protection to the organization and the volunteer in case of accidents involving autos not owned by the organization but operated by an individual engaged in organizational activities. Usually effective only after the limits of the owner's own policy have been exceeded.

Umbrella Coverage--increasing the normal limits of policies in case of an unusual, disaster-type situation. Sometimes referred to as the Million Dollar Umbrella.

There are many variations on these coverages depending on the state and the policy. Appropriateness of type and amount of coverage will be determined by the nature of the organization and the work being performed. For example, transporting children carries a different risk than picking up and delivering supplies. Although we have defined operational volunteers as staff for functional purposes, they are not eligible for workers' compensation. In considering insurance, every effort should be made to reduce any extraordinary risk which the volunteer may be taking.

Of growing interest to policy volunteers is a relative newcomer to the insurance scene: directors' and officers' liability insurance, often referred to as D & O. Since it is new and does pertain to points made in earlier chapters, it seems appropriate to give it more than a nod here.

Most state laws permit corporations (including nonprofit) to indemnify board members for loss sustained from actions brought against them for wrongful acts. That is, an organization may reimburse its directors for costs incurred in a suit provided that the director acted in good faith. Particularly for nonprofit organizations there is an important difference between being permitted to reimburse and being able to. Hence the availability of insurance permits an organization to back up its commitment of indemnification with the resources to pay for it.

164

Depending on state laws, organization bylaws, and specific insurance policies, definitions of what constitutes a wrongful act will vary. However, "wrongful act" never includes being dishonest or gaining financial profit or other personal advantage unfairly by virtue of one's position as a director. These acts are simply wrong and the perpetrator personally responsible. Wrongful acts for which a board member MIGHT be held liable are those which result in harm to the corporation and its assets, its creditors, or members of the public and MAY come under such headings as waste, extravagance, mismanagement, neglect, unfair labor practices, and violation of organization bylaws.

When allegations are made, the review of the facts will include examination of "good faith." The court will be looking at whether or not the person under fire exercised "reasonable" care, skill and prudence in performing duties, i.e., took such steps as:

--attending board and committee meetings and insisting that meetings be meaningful

--reading materials before signing or voting on them

--knowing and acting in accordance with the organization's basic documents and applicable local, state, and Federal laws

--registering dissent and/or getting any potential conflict of interest on the record

--getting and using sound information and, when necessary, seeking outside professional advice.

In the eyes of the law, directors have a fiduciary responsibility regarding the organizations they serve. They have been entrusted to carry out a publicly useful purpose through a private, nonprofit organization. They violate this trust not only when they are not honest but also when they are not conscientious. Being a figurehead or a rubberstamp is always unacceptable philosophically, as we saw in Chapter 6. It may also be risky financially, since D & O insurance is not designed to cover this type of poor performance.

While D & O liability insurance is now available and has its attractions, it has some drawbacks as well. It represents an extra cost (probably in the neighborhood of at least $1000 per year) which the organization may not be able to justify in light of its budget situation. Also a policy may require co-insurance by the individual director or may have a large deductible ($1000-$2500) on the front end of any claims for which the organization or the individual is responsible. D & O shares with all liability insurance the likelihood that, if it is known this coverage is in effect, plaintiffs are more likely to include individual directors in any suit against the organization and the courts are more apt to make awards. If more organizations buy this insurance and if more claims against it result, the cost will become increasingly prohibitive, and a vicious cycle will keep spinning. Heads they win; tails you lose except that we all lose when these problems arise, insured or not.

As for insurance in general, even though certain types of coverage are available and even though in principle volunteers should be protected from unusual risk, it does not necessarily follow that the responsible organization will buy everything just in case. It can be expected, however, to investigate all of the options with the advice of professional insurance personnel and to provide whatever protection is reasonable and appropriate in the organization and in the particular geographic area. Having done this, it can assure those of its volunteers who are performing in an accountable fashion that they may continue to do so without undue fear. Conversely, an organization can point out to those recalcitrant volunteers who do not want to be "hemmed in" by a lot of red tape that by not acting accountably they are putting themselves at risk as well as being less than useful to the organization. As we have seen, there are many good reasons to build a sense of accountability into volunteer performance. But if all else fails, the insurance-related argument may get people's attention.

A positive trend in volunteering today is the growing recognition that some skills and work habits acquired and/or demonstrated in volunteer work add significantly to the qualifications which a potential employee can submit when applying for a paid position and which a prospective employer would do well to consider. Though appropriate community service work has long been recognized as job related for rising corporate executives, it has come as quite a surprise to many that volunteering has career development aspects.

As women began re-entering the work force, many of them discovered that their premarriage and prefamily paid experience was not by itself readily marketable, and they began to wonder what exactly they had been doing with their lives in that ten- to twenty-year interval. In many instances they had performed as volunteers in positions of substance and responsibility and felt that their "employment" history and present employability were greater than could be shown on the job application forms they were being asked to fill out. Thus began a protest and a campaign which are beginning to benefit all volunteers and to offer a way for society to acknowledge that work done by volunteers is as real and important as any other. The campaign needs to proceed on two fronts.

First we must teach volunteers who are new to job-seeking maneuvers how to translate their volunteer experiences into job-hunting jargon. To do this, an organization should start by making sure that volunteers have job titles and job definitions. Then it might incorporate into its support system some written examples from the work in that organization and some suggested general resources for help in resume writing. Letters of reference from various organizational contacts may well be appropriate. The organization should also practice what it preaches and ensure that its own pre-employment forms allow for applicants to provide this information.

A gentle caution should be inserted for the inexperienced pointing out that for a volunteer experience to be applicable, it needs to be relevant to the job being applied for. Some resume-writing guidelines tend to get carried away with translating everything into snappy buzz words which are quickly seen through in personnel offices. Also the popular literature often features success stories of the "How I Turned My Volunteering into a $50,000 Job!" variety which inspire visions of sugar plums among those new to the labor market. Ten years of stuffing envelopes monthly may say something about reliability. But no amount of semantic gymnastics can make it a qualification for a middle-management position, even if one is forty and does not want to start at the bottom. Coordinating a team of clerical or program volunteers might be a different story.

Secondly, prospective employers need to be made more aware that they have something to gain by considering an applicant's total work record and not just the paid experience portion. Right now that is often the task of the individual volunteer/job seeker, for many companies' employment applications do not invite much information on this. Two or three lines for relevant community service may not do justice to the professional skills acquired by some people in their volunteer work and, even if every inch is used, still have a negative visual impact juxtaposed with the larger open space allowed for employment experience. It may take a carefully drafted cover letter and an assertive interview to bring this into proper perspective.

Private companies have not been the only "villains" in this piece. Government job application forms and procedures have done little better. Many states are revising civil service hiring practices to collect and make use of this information. In New York, this move may have been hastened along by a law suit in which the plaintiff argued that by excluding this data the state discriminated against women because women do more volunteer work than men. The Division of Human Rights agreed. Henceforth the state's Civil Service Department will count volunteer work as part of applicants' experience and will credit it to the extent such experience would be accepted if paid. However, the department was not ordered to reconsider the plaintiff for the job, nor did the decision cover local civil service positions.[2]

It is to be hoped that a glut of law suits will not be required to promote this aspect of volunteering. If we are on the lookout for them, we may each have opportunities to raise the subject in conversation. We might also point up the problem within our own places of employment, share successes and failures in our own networks, and support such lobbying efforts as are necessary so the idea that volunteering can contribute to an individual's work record becomes less and less novel.

Keep in mind that the relevance of this to effective volunteering in the present is not to stroke the volunteers and say, "Thanks! I guess we owe you something." It is to acknowledge that good performance and training are good performance and training regardless of whether they have been paid for in dollars or not. Volunteer work can be evaluated, accepted, and rejected on those terms.

8.6 THE APRIL 15 RECOGNITION

Interestingly, the Federal income tax laws have not done too bad a job in giving recognition to the work volunteers do and the costs they incur. From the inception of the income tax in 1917, recognition has been given to the fact that some work being done by private, nonprofit organizations serves the common good in a unique and important way and that if this work were not being done by these private groups, government would probably have to see that it was done and pay for it with tax dollars. Thus it was deemed to be in the public interest to reduce the tax burden on donors for monies contributed privately to these organizations; hence the concept of the charitable deduction.

Included in definitions of what constitutes a contribution are some of the out-of-pocket expenses associated with volunteer work for public as well as private, nonprofit organizations.[3] At the moment these include:

--Amounts paid for transportation from home to the place where you serve

--Automobile expenses--gas and oil, parking, tolls--in getting to and from the volunteer work as well as during the work time

--Reasonable payment for necessary meals and lodging while away from home overnight

--If an elected convention delegate, expenses for travel, transportation, reasonable amounts for meals and lodging while away from home overnight

--Costs of stamps, stationery, refreshments, supplies used specifically for the organization

--Long-distance calls on organization business

--Uniforms

But it is not just volunteers who sometimes mean well and do not quite measure up, and there are some hitches in these deductions. First volunteers who drive are allowed to deduct the actual costs of gas and oil or may take a standard mileage rate. That rate, though it has increased over the years, is substantially less than the one allowed for business driving. The volunteer mileage rate is not intended to cover auto-related expenses such as insurance, maintenance and depreciation. The assumption is that these are expenses the individual would incur anyway and therefore do not constitute a charitable contribution. On the positive side, volunteers can count miles driven to and from as well as during their volunteer work whereas an employee is not allowed to deduct the costs of getting to and from the job. Nevertheless, the discrepancy between volunteer and busines rates is large enough to warrant further examination of the rationale.

Secondly, permissible deductions do not include childcare or meals involved when one is in town, though, as we saw earlier, such expenses may not in fact be normally incurred and are directly attributable to one's volunteer work.

Thirdly, deductions are permitted only if made to organizations recognized by the Internal Revenue Service as charitable. Thus it is possible that someone doing lots of good works may not get tax breaks if the organization does not qualify or if the individual works informally and alone. This is not an unjustified "hitch" but is something to check out if there is any question.

Finally the biggest inequity has been that the only taxpayer/donor/volunteers who could get a tax break were those who itemize their deductions on the long form. This has meant that these benefits accrued to the more affluent. This has become even more true as the standard deduction allowed to all taxpayers has been increased, and more people have opted to use the short form. The deduction approach to charitable giving when combined with the increased standard deduction has had a profoundly detrimental effect on charitable giving in general, and, where volunteers are concerned, has excluded larger numbers and a wider cross section from receiving this tangible recognition of their efforts.

A major breakthrough on this issue was made with the Economic Recovery Tax Law of 1981 which provided for the introduction of tax credits for charitable contributions beginning in 1982. This will mean that, for the first time, taxpayers who do not itemize deductions will get above-the-line credit for contributions including out-of-pocket volunteer expenses.

The immediate impact of this is more conceptual than practical because the credit system will be implemented in stages and within limits. The amount taken off for donations will be a percentage of total contributions not to exceed a total amount or "cap" for the first three years. It applies as follows:[4]

YEAR	PERCENTAGE	CAP	MAXIMUM DEDUCTION
1982	25	$100	$25
1983	25	$100	$25
1984	25	$300	$75
1985	50	None	Half of all given
1986	100	None	All given

After 1986 the provision expires and must be renewed. Nonetheless it is a step in the right direction.

Here again action to assure that this form of support for volunteering is kept heading in the right direction will need to take place on two fronts. First we can make sure that individual volunteers know if their organization qualifies them for tax breaks and, if so, what expenses count as contributions. They need to remember to document their expenses and mileage, to count only those which are allowed and are directly attributable to doing the volunteer work, and NOT to count those expenses for which they have been reimbursed. It may be particularly important to offer this information to volunteers with the introduction of the tax credit concept because those who have not itemized deductions may have had little practice in taking full advantage of their rightful tax benefits. Those forms can get pretty formidable. Also many volunteers have not gotten into the habit of keeping proper records for this kind of tax purpose.

Secondly, we will need to stay alert to remaining inequities and unanswered questions which will have to be thrashed out in the political arena. Is the volunteer/business mileage differential justified? Can other expenses such as meals and childcare be considered contributions? Has the credit concept worked? Should it be renewed? Do state and local income taxes give proper recognition to volunteer expenses? We can take heart in these struggles from the recent breakthrough on tax credits for charitable contributions. That was a change brought about by a long, sustained, informed, and energetic lobbying effort by various organizations in the private voluntary sector with the support of sympathetic legislators and government leaders.[5]

8.7 VOLUNTEERING: THE CAUSE AND SOME UNFINISHED BUSINESS

In most settings the status of volunteers is a secondary concern. The organizations exist and the volunteers are attracted to them because of specific substantive concerns about human welfare, human dignity, and social justice which have nothing direct to do with volunteering per se. In these settings, volunteers are perceived as a means to an end and rightly so if the end is meeting the mutually perceived human need and if the volunteers are increasingly incorporated into full and effective partnership with other personnel. We will have done a great deal to promote volunteering if, within existing organizations, we stop lumping volunteers into one faceless, do-gooding category and start recognizing the differences not only among volunteers as human beings but among volunteer roles.

It must be clear by now, however, that in some instances it is useful to treat volunteering as The Cause and to encourage those organizations whose mission as well as whose method is volunteerism. Some volunteer-related issues require time, energy and money expenditures beyond the capacity of organizations and individuals whose main concentration is another social concern.

Many communities have Voluntary Action Centers or Volunteer Bureaus, whose services may include being a clearinghouse and referral system for all kinds of volunteer opportunities, initiating and co-ordinating volunteer training events, disseminating information and sponsoring activities which promote volunteerism. Some states have Offices of Citizen Participation or agency with a similar name and function. At the national level there are numerous groups grappling with different pieces of the big picture. A small sample of these include:

ACTION-- a Federal agency to encourage citizen participation. Umbrella organization which has among other things sponsored Peace Corps, VISTA, RSVP and Foster Grandparents

VOLUNTEER: The National Center for Citizen Involvement--a private organization formed in 1979 by the merger of the National Center for Voluntary Action and the National Information Center on Volunteerism

Association of Volunteer Administration--concerned with defining professional base and standards for volunteer administrators

Association of Junior Leagues--an organization
which promotes volunteerism by demonstrating the effectiveness of trained
volunteers

Alliance for Volunteerism--a consortium of national
voluntary organizations which have local
units. Focuses on improving communication
and collaboration among members at
national and local levels.

These and other groups engage in advocacy,
research, demonstration projects, preparation and dis-
semination of materials, and nationwide volunteer
recognition/promotion activities. They are organizations which rely on various configurations of public and
private funding, and thus they are subject to the
vicissitudes of organizational maintenance. Nor are
they immune from the problems of achieving effectiveness
which we have been discussing. Nonetheless, they are
pulling together a lot of important information and are
creating networks within volunteerism and between the
voluntary sector and other segments of society. This
should ultimately enhance the status of volunteers and
strengthen the structures where volunteers are at work
or are needed. Recent examples include joint conferences between the Association of Junior Leagues and the
National Association of Social Workers to explore
staff/volunteer concerns and a VOLUNTEER-sponsored
Wingspread symposium bringing together leaders from the
corporate and nonprofit sectors to explore current and
future efforts of corporations to encourage employee
volunteering.

When the results of volunteer advocacy reach other
volunteer organizations in the form of how-to-do-it-
better guidelines, shared success stories or legislative
changes, it is easy to appreciate what these organizations are doing. Sometimes their activities will seem
at best to be symbolic and ceremonial pep rallies whose
success or failure is hard to evaluate until time has
been allowed for their effects to trickle down to the
grass roots. At other times the burning issues
occupying volunteer advocates may seem about as compelling as determining how many angels sit on the head
of a pin. Yet some of the important issues to be
considered are:

--Defining volunteer

--Counting volunteers and measuring the scope of volunteering. (Related issue: If volunteering is so important to society, why was it not counted in the 1980 Census? Shall we try for 1990?)

--Putting a dollar value on volunteer time. Should it be done? If so, should it be at a uniform rate such as minimum wage or at some other economic estimate of the value of work performed? Is it applicable only to operations volunteering? How should the information be used? As in-kind income for grant-seeking purposes? As a morale booster for volunteers?

--Analyzing media images of volunteering, reinforcing the good ones and trying to eliminate the negative ones

--Developing curricula for students which might provide volunteer opportunities to explore career options and/or to promote the idea of volunteering as an important component of responsible citizenship

--Incorporating employee volunteering into the total definition of a corporation's expression of its corporate citizenship

--Establishing a code of ethics for volunteers and promoting professional training and standards for volunteer administrators.

Each of these has complex ramifications philosophically and practically. There are many intellectual and political quags in which to get mired. Yet there is more in each of these than fodder for an interesting discussion or a doctoral dissertation. There is the possibility of redefining and refining our understanding of realities in volunteering with hard data and hard thinking rather than reinforcing mushy, romantic myths about The Volunteer.

While the advocates of volunteerism will not be automatically more effective than any other group of concerned citizens, it behooves all of us who are concerned with volunteering to recognize the validity of these issues and to keep abreast of developments around them so that we can make informed and appropriate responses to specific requests for action and support. We do not have to make careers out of volunteerism to encourage those who do. Occasional letters to legislators and editors and periodic participation in community volunteer recognition pushes will not divert individuals and organizations from their "real" issues. Rather they are examples of the kinds of small, economical activities whose cumulative effect when multiplied nationwide will be positive for volunteerism and ultimately positive for individual volunteers.

REFERENCES

[1]Vern Lake, "101 Ways to Give Recognition to Volunteers," VOLUNTARY ACTION LEADERSHIP, Winter, 1977, pp. 13-14.

[2]THE NEW YORK TIMES, August 7, 1980, III 13:3.

[3]U.S. Department of the Treasury, Internal Revenue Service, "Charitable Contributions," Publication No. 526, Revised November, 1981.

[4]U.S. Department of the Treasury, Internal Revenue Service, "Highlights of 1981 Tax Changes," Publication No. 553, Revised December, 1981.

[5]THE CONGRESSIONAL RECORD, Senate, Vol. 127, No. 10, January 20, 1981.

SECTION III

EFFECTIVE VOLUNTEERING:

PERSPECTIVES FOR THE FUTURE

9

VISION VOLUNTEERING

9.1   WHAT IF . . . .?

We now have a sweeping perspective on the historical context which has shaped volunteering, and we now
have some perspective on strengths and weaknesses,
opportunities and pitfalls in volunteering today. We
have ranged from the panoramic to the picayune in our
stated commitment to examine volunteering in all its
complexity. Now what if we had gained sufficient
information, insight, and inspiration from this essen-
tially intellectual exercise to try to implement the
action ideas found in this book and elsewhere? Would we
have accomplished what we wanted to? Would there have
been some unintended, less desirable consequences? The

answer is yes to both questions, and the questions and answers can be looked at on at least two levels.

First let us continue with the assumptions underlying Section II that much volunteering takes place in organizations and that those organizations are in fact promoting some important facet of human welfare, human dignity, and social justice. Application of concepts such as volunteering as work not play, sound personnel management, and mutual accountability should put us well down the road to greater efficiency. They will enable us to operate with greater clarity of purpose and function and will help us maximize our individual and collective contributions to whatever concern we are mobilized to address. If expectations and rewards are mutually understood, if all partners in the venture are respected, and if there is a better fit between individual and organizational needs, we cannot help but see improved performance. It is quite possible also that greater volunteer satisfaction will promote greater reliability, longer-term commitments and better public relations.

Yet even in the present these factors may have counterproductive consequences. The overzealous reformer who takes all the suggested motions seriously may find that too much of even a good thing becomes as much a problem as the myths and traditions which have impeded volunteers in the past. For example, a masterful, impassioned interpretation of the joys of accountability to a board of directors may scare people to death.

A recruitment appeal emphasizing "Look what's in it for you" may attract individual volunteers to certain tasks for a time. But will an overdose of the personal and career development aspects sustain that commitment if the volunteer is only lukewarm about the cause being served? If the main reason for volunteering is "what's in it for me," then what distinguishes doing volunteer work from participating in the neighborhood tennis tournament or taking a job-related course to enhance one's career position?

More realistic structuring of the requirements for volunteer jobs to acknowledge the limits on the

volunteers' available time will be fairer to all parties
involved. However, it also encourages an ad hoc
mentality which says, "Here is the activity/problem of
the week; let us get it taken care of and be done with
it." This diverts attention from determining whether,
if all the pieces were done, they would add up to
something. This is particularly threatening to the
effective functioning of policy volunteers whose job it
is to look at bigger pictures over longer periods of
time yet where the ad hoc committee is terribly
fashionable.

To be honest, few if any of these unintended and
more negative-sounding consequences are intolerable or
unmanageable for the present. Looking at worst cases,
is a board immobilized by fear of individual liability
any worse than one ensnared by groupthink? The former
may even be easier to overcome because it is more
overt. If particular operational tasks get done, does
it matter if the volunteers did it because they owed
someone a favor instead of because they "really
cared?" Does it matter if we have enticed/inspired as
opposed to conned/manipulated if the outcome was some
good accomplished? Probably not--in the short run.

However, what if we need to challenge the assumption that the organizations which currently exist,
however efficiently they operate, are in fact reducing
or eliminating problems of human welfare, human dignity,
and social justice? What if we capitalize on all the
positives and minimize the negatives in volunteerism? Will we automatically have, in addition to armies
of happy, efficient volunteers doing "good works," a
collective impact which makes society more responsive to
the needs of its individual members?

There are those whose political or religious
convictions provide them with a clear picture of the
ideal society. If these groups were in charge of the
world, we would not need to worry about who should be
doing what, for they could tell us precisely and, given
the chance and the power, would gladly do so.

There are others including this writer who believe
that in a democratic, pluralistic society there is no
one eternal and absolute set of standards for measuring

when we have arrived at complete equity and justice, that definitions and perspectives on what constitutes human welfare and dignity are always relative and varied. Our definitions and measurements are partly a function of knowledge we have about the nature of problems and the results of previous attempts at solutions. That knowledge is changing and expanding and should help us refine our notions of doing good. However, the perspectives from which we determine ultimate success remain in the realm of individual value judgments.

The crazy quilt design by which society responds to the needs of its members represents our collective value judgment at any one time. That it has proved inadequate or incomplete is evident in the constant changes which it undergoes. Today's crazy quilt/status quo is not necessarily a more definitive solution than yesterday's was or tomorrow's will be. There are times when it seems to have little to recommend it, particularly now that the frontier seems to have slammed shut. There are times when those, including volunteers, who are trying to play an active role in shaping today's design or even a modest piece of it begin to wonder if it is worth the bother. In other words, as an end product the crazy quilt has failed.

What if we view the crazy quilt as a process, albeit cumbersome? What if we view the end product, albeit abstract, as a society whose members are free to pursue life, liberty and happiness in ways which assure their individual autonomy and release their full potential without tromping on the rights of others? Are there continuing, unique and positive roles which volunteers can play to move us toward the ideal? Can we take what we have learned from the history of volunteering, put it with the strategies which we know will make volunteers more effective today and come up with an approach which will lay the groundwork for effective volunteering in the future?

There are grounds for optimism on these questions if the groundwork is properly laid. There are four dimensions which such a groundwork would contain and which must be understood and emphasized by those committed to both the present and the future:

--Promoting volunteer liberation

--Appealing to enlightened self-interest

--Developing alternate structures

--Cultivating vision volunteers

9.2 PROMOTING VOLUNTEER LIBERATION

Volunteers per se are not generally perceived as one of the world's oppressed or unliberated groups. Who if not American volunteers have felt and been freer to do what they please? Are they not already free from some risks because they can choose to act in ways which do not threaten their livelihood? Have we not just spent considerable time harping about volunteers needing to be more accountable and a little less free-wheeling? Of what use in a discussion of volunteerism is a trendy word like liberation?

Recalling our definitions and our historical review, volunteers are those citizens who believe that something is out of kilter between individuals and society and believe they have an obligation and an opportunity to do something about it now. They do not believe they should sit back and let nature take its course. For whatever reason, volunteers do not feel powerless to effect change. They choose to get involved and to give the perceived problem their best shot within the constraints of their time, energy, knowledge and skills.

We have also seen that, while society has given lip service to volunteer involvement as an admirable form of responsible citizenship, quieter forces have operated which have unnecessarily restricted the volunteers from making full contribution of such resources as they are willing to give. Much of what we have already discussed falls in this category: assignment of roles by sex and social class; derogatory designation of volunteers as amateurs, nonexperts, and dabblers; a scaling down of many volunteer tasks to the level of busy work; measurement of individual worth by the work done for pay; and discounting of other activities as play. All of these reduce the individual volunteers' sense of personal worth and potential.

Yet if we carry our reaction to these forces too far, we may add new burdens to the volunteers such as defending their "professionalism." Will a given cause be better served if everyone becomes too "valuable" or "dignified" to lick the stamps? Pseudoprofessional snobbery and insecurity, however understandable its source, will be no more attractive on volunteers than it is on staff. Will too much career development marketing raise the cost of the risk taking already inherent in volunteering? Would the use of stipends free some groups to volunteer without introducing new strings, not the least of which might be dependence on additional income?

To be sure, much of what we have discussed will be liberating to many volunteers because it will help define and refine their options for service in this complex age and will help increase chances that their best shot will make a positive difference, at least to the extent of what we now know. Properly understood, accountability will release volunteers from the burden of being either priceless or worthless, from feeling the need to be all things to all people all the time, and for doing the best they can on those concerns they believe are urgent. "Accountability" can serve as a gentle or harsh reminder that liberation is not license to do what strikes one's fancy and that totally unbridled or exclusively hit-and-miss anything is at best counterproductive and quite possibly destructive to servers as well as the served. There is an important difference between being free to do what you deem prudent and what you darn please.

CAUTION: VOLUNTEER LIBERATION MAY BE HAZARDOUS TO HEALTH.

The one big problem which even the most balanced use of professionalism and accountability will not resolve is that dark cloud over volunteering, unreliability. We have already seen that this is a many-faceted phenomenon and that the term has been applied to individual volunteers sometimes fairly but just as often unfairly.

Given what we know at present about the nature of social problems and about what increases the effectiveness and satisfaction of individuals who wish to be involved, it is both legitimate and desirable to discourage gadfly volunteering. However, given what we do NOT know, the collective impact of volunteer choices and volunteer mobility gives us many clues about whether our systems are working, what issues of human welfare are still perceived as unresolved, and where those who are willing to volunteer believe they will find the most effectiveness and satisfaction. Sorting out the significance of the clues may produce headaches and ulcers, but it is essential in order to insure that volunteering as a mechanism is not co-opted by the society which it purports to improve or enrich.

9.3   APPEALING TO ENLIGHTENED SELF-INTEREST

We have surmounted one obstacle to effective volunteering: the notion that "true" volunteers have no ulterior or selfish motives and that their actions are purely altruistic. Indeed the halo of moral superiority which has hovered over volunteering can produce many problems such as arrogance among those who enjoy feeling superior and embarrassment among those who have discovered they "enjoy" some volunteer work more than others even if all the causes are equally valid. We are able now to acknowledge that we can help ourselves when we help others and furthermore that, if we are not helping ourselves when we help others, we may accomplish less than we would like. The professional volunteer trend has greatly improved our ability to create a better fit between the needs and skills of individual volunteers and the performance requirements of the organizations in which they may work by appealing to and accomodating the volunteers' self-interest.

It has led us, however, to gloss over a component of that self-interest which may be the most critical factor in determining the effectiveness of the volunteers: a commitment to the cause which inspired the individual to volunteer instead of doing something else. It is possible to be so preoccupied with writing job descriptions and making volunteer working conditions appealing that we forget this will not attract and hold

184

volunteers if in the first place they do not have some kernel of concern about the issue being addressed.

How can commitment to a cause be considered a form of self-interest? On the surface it smacks more of the nobility hype we have been trying to counteract. However, let us recall that volunteers are those citizens who not only see a given social condition as a problem or opportunity in the abstract but who also take it personally. For any number of reasons, articulated or not, they feel a personal sense of responsibility to act. If this characteristic is part of their personality make-up, it is in their self-interest to find an outlet for this urge to become involved.

Underlying this urge is the conviction that in some way and to varying degrees members of a society are interrelated and that what affects one ultimately affects all. This conviction also makes it in one's self-interest to become involved, as a kind of self-defense if nothing else. These two dimensions of perceived social responsibility are often expressed in one breath with such phrases as:

--It is my duty to be charitable now even if my reward is not in this life.

--Since I have been in those shoes, I must help others.

--If I had that problem, I would want help, and the problem could happen to me.

--That experience meant a lot to me as a child; I owe it to this generation.

--I want to show love for neighbor. My neighbors are those who live next door, in the same town, across the nation, or anywhere in the world where this condition exists.

--If we do not solve this problem, we will all suffer economically, physically, emotionally and/or spiritually.

NOTE: To call the actions which result from these perceptions "self-interest" may be factual. However, to call them "enlightened" is a value judgement made by those of us who already believe that "no man is an island" and who already believe that discontent, anger, desire for progress AND action are the ways human nature takes its course. We may be wrong, but on the off chance we are right, we might as well make the best of it.

Commitment to a cause is influenced partly by an enlightened self-interest, i.e., a perception that one has some kind of personal stake. But commitment is also shaped by one's assessment of what if any impact one's actions will have on a perceived problem. It is one thing to see a problem and understand that it affects you and quite another to believe that you can do something about it. In fact our definitions of what conditions are problems are often shaped by our ability to see solutions. This happens because the personal price of looking at problems which seem to defy solution is too high. For example, it is easier to "see" hunger in the destitute family up the street than to cope with mass starvation in Africa. If you decide that the least and the most you can do about the latter is to send a check and then you learn how badly the relief agency bungles administration, there is little left to do except weep. If the harm is being done but our attempts at doing good are not working, what is the point of investing time, energy, and money? Tilting at windmills for the sake of tilting at windmills is not intrinsically rewarding for most people.

Effective volunteers are those people who have sensed several dimensions of a particular problem and for whom these dimensions have come into focus at a particular time in such a way as to compel them to act:

Perception of a problem or challenge as existing
Perception of it as affecting them
Perception of a solution which they can help bring about
Perception of a time frame in which that solution may be expected
Perception that costs of seeing and acting are not only affordable but are outweighed by the personal benefits of involvement

186

Unfortunately--or perhaps fortunately, this awareness and focusing do not occur on the same issues at the
same level for all volunteers at the same time except in
some emergency situations. Nor do these factors automatically come together to support lifelong dedication
by any one person to a single task or cause. As if this
were not confusing enough, the focal point of commitment
for an individual can change if any one of the
dimensions changes. Obviously this "focus factor" can
be used to explain the obvious. It may seem to
obfuscate it by providing a pseudoclassy description of
everything from total noninvolvement to martyrdom. Yet
a closer look provides grounds for cautious optimism AND
action.

First the good news. At the top of that list is
the fact that the components of self-interest ever
combine to produce action at all. A lot of "do-gooding"
time and energy has been spent bemoaning that most
people only get involved in a crisis, and we have not
understood the implications of this on volunteer service
for the long haul. It is in times of emergency that
people can visualize problems, solutions and ending
points for their involvement. This is true whether the
crisis is a natural or human disaster. We do not need
to conduct a sociological experiment to prove that you
might poll the neighborhood vigorously one week
searching for a Scout leader and getting only emphatic
or apologetic "nos" whereas if you contacted the same
people the next week announcing an organizational
meeting to protest the building of a nuclear power plant
down the road, you would for a time have volunteers
coming out of your ears. What the crisis response
suggests is that most people can be sparked into action
if they can "see" the urgency and opportunities for
personal response. It is not a matter of finding the
unselfish ones but of selling the urgency and potential
of less dramatic causes and not assuming everyone can
"see" the problem.

The second basis for optimism and action engendered
by this focusing business is that the focus is not
static. In the above-mentioned crisis situations, most
people will regroup at the level of business as
usual. However, some will not! Some will have gained
from the crisis a new perspective on the problem and

187

will be willing to pursue the next "obvious" solution, particularly if asked. For example, a flood may be an act of God. Yet some may perceive that consequences of the flood could have been less dire if the disaster-relief agencies had been better equipped to respond. Others may conclude that the government should have built that dam instead of abandoning it on the drawing board. In either case, their recent experience and their assessment of it may well lead them to new kinds of volunteer work. The lingering memory of the actual crisis may be a significant part of what sustains them for some time. However, its importance in motivation may diminish as they encounter new problems, new challenges, and new rewards.

Furthermore, not everyone becomes committed to a given issue by having had direct experience with it. One does not have to be an unwed mother to understand that problem and yet for any number of reasons one can still find that this issue is the one which hits in a personal way and compels involvement. Having this indirect perspective and commitment does not necessarily mean that one is smarter, more moral, more selfless or even more objective. Nor does it mean that one is automatically less understanding of the "real" problem, more self-righteous, self-serving or patient. Whether the initial prompting was from direct experience or less direct exposure, people will vary--thank heaven--in what tasks they are willing to perform and at what level of abstraction or geography. There are individuals in a position to volunteer to improve food distribution in starving countries. Just because this might entail meetings in Switzerland does not mean the work being done is any more or less passionate, difficult, and effective than delivering a food basket on the other side of town.

Finally the dynamics of focusing and refocusing suggest a wealth of opportunity for improving recruitment practices. Greater sensitivity to the several facets of volunteers' perceptions would give those already involved the opportunity to help shape these perceptions not by hitting the prospective volunteer with a 2x4 but by providing better information and support to individuals during their decision making.

A good recruitment process requires actively seeking people out and trying to get as well as give the right information. The process covers such ground as:

1. Here is why we believe this issue/problem is important to all of us. Do you feel that way too?

2. If so, here are the solutions we are working on. Do they make sense to you?

3. If so, we feel that you have much to offer and, given your particular skills, interest and availability, these are the pieces of the action you might find worthwhile. Do they appeal?

4. If so, we can place you in an assignment and give you training and supervision to help orient you or help overcome gaps and fears to increase your confidence and skills. This will also help you through the rough times and help speed up the "payback" time. How 'bout it?

5. If no to any of the above, thank you for your consideration of our offer. Best wishes with whatever you choose to do as a volunteer elsewhere.

If this list sounded phony, wait until the first time a prospect replies, "No, the various components of my self-interest are not focused on this issue/task at this time." Phony or not, it would be a substantial improvement over the "of course you'd love this" or "I don't suppose I could talk you into . . ." approaches to recruitment. Remember too that this would be much less stilted and patronizing when phrased around a particular cause, when conveyed with the recruiter's own warmth and zeal, and when practiced enough to make the recruiter more comfortable with the questions and more aware that "no" is often the right answer.

CAUTION: ENLIGHTENMENT MAY BE HAZARDOUS TO HEALTH, if for no other reason than that it can be exhausting. Individuals who are predisposed to volunteer are apt to be aware of many problems and to have some concept of civic duty. Saying "yes" too often leads to dabbling and fatigue. These persons are inclined to fall for the sloppy recruitment approach of "you really OUGHT TO" because they see why that argument is correct and feel guilty if they do not WANT to. Also for these individuals refocusing can be a tense time particularly if it means abandoning one ship to board another. It is the rare situation where the individual is applauded for moving from one good cause to another.

Recruiters can be worn down by a sense of failure if they cannot convince the first person or even the first five that the particular volunteer job opening is an offer which cannot be refused. One healthy and productive "yes" does not always seem to make up for the many rejections, and the long haul is hard to keep in the forefront of one's thinking. Yet too many guilt trips and too many unsatisfactory placements invite a mutual writing off of volunteering by all parties involved. That would not be in anyone's enlightened self-interest.

Organizations tend to do most of their recruiting for limited, immediate needs. All too often, recruiters are only equipped to promote one or two of the many positions which might be available in a given organization. Often they compete with other recruiters within the same organization as well as with those from other groups. This should become less of a problem if we can make better use of internal co-ordination, centralized volunteer agencies or of informal interorganizational referrals.

Nothing we have said so far simplifies the individual's decision making or eases the ongoing, hard work which recruitment is, so there is no sense spending our energy moaning and groaning. We have to take the risk that greater self-awareness and intentionality are worth the trouble. Then we can settle in for the long haul and move on to insuring the availability of appropriate structures to receive those who choose to get involved.

9.4 DEVELOPING ALTERNATE STRUCTURES

With all the unfinished and perhaps unfinishable business of building a more responsive democratic society and with the uncounted and perhaps uncountable opportunities today's crazy quilt provides for volunteer service, it is tempting to assume that having alternate structures is the least of our problems. We cannot fill all the slots as it is. To be sure, a strong part of any case for alternate structures is the need to have individual volunteers working not only on concerns they believe to be most urgent but in ways which address those concerns at the level the volunteers believe are appropriate. The personal toll of a misfit between the volunteer and the slot has already been discussed. On these grounds alone, the cumulative impact of having too many volunteers in the wrong spots at the wrong times will be negative on volunteering.

There are, however, larger societal ramifications in the collective impact of individual volunteer choices which are influenced by the availability and effectiveness of alternate structures. Any structure, like any individual, has strengths and limitations in the kind of response it can produce, and we need to appreciate the potential and the pitfalls inherent in each.

The oldest structure for American volunteering is NEIGHBORING. In the good old days it was virtually the only mechanism available to address social needs. It provided a tangible way to alleviate a perceived need or to enrich the lives of both parties. And it still does. There are many immediate and tangible acts of neighborliness by which one person or group can combat isolation, ease temporary dislocation, or simply brighten someone's day. Perhaps we have become so "sophisticated" about the complexity of individual and social problems, so protective of our own right to individual self-sufficiency and privacy, and so fearful of butting in where we are not wanted that we are ignoring close-to-home opportunities to make society a little better by making the life of a neighbor a little pleasanter or more bearable. Certainly, a would-be good neighbor runs the risk of seeing the right need the wrong way, of doing more harm than good, and/or of being rebuffed. While these possibilities should make us more cautious, sensitive, and humble, the risk is no greater and no less in neighboring than in any other form of volunteering.

The neighboring model goes beyond individual charitable acts to include the "let's pitch in" grass-roots self-help perception of problems. Here again there is often much to this approach that is valid and achievable. But a preoccupation with the neighborhood as an autonomous geographic entity can distort some realities about the nature of the problems and what it takes to solve them, as the following experiences of this writer illustrate:

While working as an agency staff member, the writer was invited to an economically depressed area by a group of neighborhood leaders who had already been cultivated by other agency staff. The assignment was to help mobilize a neighborhood cleanup project as the first step in building among the residents a sense of community and collective power to improve their lives. The project was a success because the neighbors did pitch in with unprecedented cooperation and zeal AND because the neighborhood leaders with staff support had secured the endorsement of area church and civic leaders, the promise of paint for Phase II from the major landlords, and a pledge of any garbage trucks needed from the city. Forty trucks were required to remove all the debris collected. The point is that all the ingredients were essential to the success of the project.

By contrast the writer currently lives in an affluent suburban neighborhood where the need to "pitch in" to improve the neighborhood is perceived as fund raising to increase the number of cultural programs offered at the neighborhood school. There is little willingness to consider that educational policy decisions made at national, state or even district levels ultimately have more to do with the quality of education than an occasional puppet show. There is even less understanding that volunteer energy should be invested in this policy process.

The consequences of ignoring all but the most immediate local concerns were brought home to some of the neighbors who, thanks to a corporate relocation, found themselves transferred to another part of the country where they were ill-prepared to understand or deal with the serious school desegregation problems of their new location. Some who became concerned and looked around reported that they were surprised to find that the same organization for which they had run bake sales had been hard at work for years trying to ease community tensions and to improve public education. While it had not been totally successful, it had kept matters from being even worse. For those who stayed put in the old neighborhood, the attention-getting crisis may not come until the next contract negotiations.

Perhaps the biggest distortion of the neighboring model is the extrapolation from the fact that some problems, risks and rewards are tangible and immediate to a belief that all of them are and if some problems are simple cases of temporary and isolated personal inadequacy, all problems are probably that at rock bottom. These are attractive but unrealistic ideas. However, if this is the prevailing perception in a particular group, it puts considerable social pressure on everyone to think "neighborhood" only. This causes those who perceive that many and more urgent problems are found outside the neighborhood to question their perceptions. Instead of saying that they believe these other issues are more important and compelling, these folks are more likely to try to do the "neighborly" thing first and then whatever they have time and energy to do on the other issues, thereby reducing their impact on and satisfaction with both.

Finally, the preoccupation with neighborhood invites an insidious form of political manipulation by those in positions of power who would like very much to have everyone so busy feeling responsible for brightening the corner where they are that they have no time and energy left to question the systems and policies which may be contributing to the problems. Of course, this ploy can backfire. One outcome of neighboring may well be a greater understanding of its limits and a shift in perception which makes neighboring a springboard to action at other levels of involvement.

We have already examined at length the next oldest structure for volunteering: the ORGANIZATION, be it public or private. We have seen how and where organizational structure and function can facilitate or impede individual volunteer action. On the positive side it provides a framework for action and continuity and is an indispensable societal tool for focusing and sustaining the application of human and material resources to problems which exceed the capacity of individuals to solve.

However, because it institutionalizes certain definitions of problems and solutions and becomes a body of more or less like-minded individuals, it develops a corporate perception which has the same limiting and liberating possibilities that individual perceptions do. It is in the enlightened self-interest of the organization not only to do well with its piece of a larger social need but to convince its members and the community at large that it is providing "the" best solution to the entire concern. This provides a powerful collective justification for equating the meeting of human needs with the insuring of organization survival and may produce blindness to clues that the equation does not balance. Call it groupthink, turf protection, or corporate blinders, it contributes to the competition for resources which characterizes organization behavior. This is not entirely unhealthy in our free enterprise society, but it becomes vicious and cut-throat under the pressures of the closed frontier. It is unhealthy in the long run when it adds another obstacle to the process of evaluating whether our individual and organizational responses to need are even optimum, let alone maximum.

Another structural setting where volunteers may get involved is the PLANNING BODY. In an effort to bring order out of the chaos inherent in a complex modern society and to take advantage of all that is useful about being scientific, businesslike, rational, and systematic, increasing numbers of concerned citizens have seen in planning an opportunity to improve the quality of the response being made by society as a whole and by specific communities or service areas. In the era of the closed frontier, the need for planning seems even more urgent because the very real problems created by insufficient resources require even greater progress in avoiding duplications, reallocating what apparently will be limited resources, and learning to set priorities.

Planning bodies provide wonderful slots for volunteers whose perception of social need and appropriate response extend beyond one issue and/or extend beyond the realm of the immediate and tangible. Unquestionably both the planning process and the resulting plans can contribute to substantial positive improvement in the way things are done, can define goals toward which to work together, and can provide a means of monitoring and measuring progress.

However, one fact which tends to get lost in the planning shuffle is that planning bodies are organizations and that they are therefore no less susceptible to the pitfalls therein than other organizations. The emphasis in planning is on cooperation, coherence, and comprehensiveness, and by definition it is more futuristic and abstract. This tempts planners to believe that their perceptions and responses represent a more enlightened form of self-interest than everyone else's and that their plans should therefore be construed as having divine authority. Even when the group has been given temporal power and authority, there are those "unenlightened" individuals and groups who choose to challenge the plan openly or to quietly not conform. Planning types then find themselves beleaguered and start reacting with motions which resemble common garden-variety groupthink and turf protection. Even if they are right that they are more enlightened, planners tend to undervalue the useful aspects of diversity, to miscalculate the strength of those forces which resist change, and to overestimate the degree to which cooperation, coherence and comprehensiveness are universally desired.

Being ever optimistic that we can find new and better ways to address concerns, another set of structures is emerging which may do a better job at capitalizing on individual and corporate diversity and still make some headway on promoting sufficient consensus and cooperation to produce results. This writer differentiates them as NETWORKING, COLLABORATION, and

COALITION. All three assume that the individual participants are wearing an organization hat of some
kind. All are predicated on the assumption that without
ignoring or stamping out individual and corporate
diversity we can identify common concerns and work on
them together or at least simultaneously. Precisely
because of the diversity, perceptions of what needs to
be done will be enriched and expanded and will generate
subsequent efforts to do something more effective. They
differ in the type of formality and accountability
required by the organizational hat.

In NETWORKING, individuals who share a common
position or assignment in their organizations meet to
share ideas and concerns, to become better informed and
then presumably to return to their organizational tasks
with greater insight and enthusiasm. Examples of groups
which might use a network are presidents and executives
of building centered agencies or program personnel of
youth recreation services. Participants implement
action ideas primarily through their own organizational
channels, and any interorganizational co-operation which
is indicated is in the form of separate but simultan-
eous, uniform but not formally united actions.

Networking is not a new societal tool, but it has
not been used much by volunteers in the course of their
volunteering. Most of it may still take place in
convention or workshop settings where "interorganizational" is apt to mean different units within the same
basic organization. Many have found that it is the
networking aspect of such gatherings which make them so
valuable. Within a given community, networking offers
considerable potential for helping individuals and
groups to be more effective and for establishing a
groundwork for other kinds of cooperation.

COLLABORATION has a little broader connotation. Its subject matter may be a single topic or a
wide-ranging sweep of community concerns. It can be a
one shot gathering or an extended series of
meetings. Its participants, even if they are "sent" by
an organization, are perceived as informally representing a constituency more than the organization
itself. The purpose is to pool the perspectives of a
wide cross section of individuals and constituencies, to

196

arrive at some consensus about problems and priorities, and to find new approaches which either strengthen or transcend existing organizational molds. A good collaboration effort unleashes considerable imagination and new or renewed energy among participants. It is most effective if it produces a plan for action and a procedure for follow-up so that participants get a sense of having accomplished something.

However, "decisions" by the collaborating group are not binding on anyone, even the organizations which sent delegates. Collaboration, like networking, is often initiated by a self-appointed individual or group, though we do not mean "self-appointed" in a pejorative sense. All this suggests is that any leverage for cooperation or change rests entirely on the creation of commitment and momentum within the collaborative group itself. This means involving both enough people and enough strategically located ones to take advantage of the good will being generated, to apply political pressure, or to use other follow-up strategies which are indicated.

In a COALITION, organizations with a common concern agree to act in a concerted way. The coalition becomes a separate entity which is empowered to act on behalf of member organizations within agreed-upon limits. Individual participants are asked to be accountable to their separate organizations by making sure the coalition does not exceed the limits of the agreement and at the same time to be accountable to the coalition by keeping their organization in tune and in time with the coalition. It does not take much imagination or experience to see that this can be an exhilarating and exasperating individual assignment, though it takes considerable imagination and experience to do a coalition job effectively. Coalitions offer organizations the opportunity to address a particular concern with a relatively economical investment of their own resources and, through the broader base and more focused action, to increase their effectiveness. Coalitions have been successfully used in advocacy, particularly legislative, where organizations who have only one issue in common can band together and make an impact. While the coalition mechanism can be cumbersome, it can also be powerful.

These three structures require a high degree of openness among participants. There must be some assurance of trust and discretion among the group and considerable respect for all that has been said about accountability as an essential ingredient in effectiveness. They present a set of alternatives which can be used to explore new levels of optimum in today's and tomorrow's crazy quilts.

CAUTION: ALTERNATE STRUCTURES MAY BE HAZARDOUS TO HEALTH.

All structures discussed have been tried. Some have failed some of the time, and others have succeeded some of the time. All have something positive to contribute, and all need to be strengthened and expanded. This leaves us still with a number of individual and corporate choices so overwhelming it can make our heads spin. It leaves us also with the paradox that, while individual and corporate blinders are essential if we are to focus on one problem long enough to accomplish anything, they are also the very reason we sometimes cannot do it.

9.5 CULTIVATING VISION VOLUNTEERS

Without backing away from previous assertions that effective volunteering requires a matching between the individual volunteer's needs and perceptions with the appropriate structured response, it is nonetheless time to suggest that a very positive contribution can be made by some kinds of misfits and that one of the most underdeveloped and underutilized groups of volunteers are those who will be described below as vision volunteers.

By vision volunteers we mean those who not only see something out of kilter in society which prompts them to get involved but who, once involved, see things out of kilter within the structures where they are operating and want to act on that too. We do not mean those individuals who are deliberately performing a fifth column function with the intent of undoing a given organization. Rather we are talking about those volunteers who believe that the given organization or system can be made more responsive.

198

These volunteers may envision specific ways to make that happen, or they may simply wonder why things are done a certain way and if they could not be done better. Their "visions" may relate to any number of levels from the "lowly" clerical volunteer who has a new idea for getting the next newsletter out to the grandiose schemer who has a different idea for how community resources should be allocated in the twenty-first century. What distinguishes these schemers from other dreamers or visionaries is that they have a desire to be involved in the process of getting from here to there. Regardless of whether their perceptions are expressed in gentle questions, modest suggestions, pointed criticisms, or angry diatribes, vision volunteers are out of sync with prevailing protocol, procedure and policy. They are seen as pests, cranks, troublemakers and rabble rousers.

The basic function of vision volunteers, whether they know it or not and whether they are in the policy or operations chain, is to question the current definitions of optimum. This is the essence of the crazy quilt process and as such can be supported enthusiastically in the abstract and over the long run. However, it certainly causes everyone discomfort in the here and now, where there is a strong need on the part of most individuals and groups to believe that they are doing the best possible job or the most that is reasonable under the circumstances. So what do "they" want? When a vision volunteer wittingly or unwittingly introduces a dissonant note, there are many ways to handle the resulting discomfort, and they can be summed up under two headings: counterproductive and productive.

Among the former are many strategies commonly employed by individuals and groups and by volunteers and staff who feel threatened by vision volunteers. Some of them are:

--Discrediting the individuals preferably by patronizing them.

e.g., What does he know? He's just a volunteer. They are too new, young, uninformed, out of it to understand.

> Poor thing! She's having trouble at work
> or at home and is taking it out on us.

--Diverting attention from the substance contained
in the question, idea or criticism and converting
the difference in perception into a personal
power struggle or a personality contest.

> e.g., When you ask that question about what we
> are doing, you are accusing me of fail-
> ure. Who are you to tell me how to do my
> job?

NOTE: These first two strategies are particularly effective when the volunteer has an
irritating personal style or other highly visible
personal quirk.

--Daring the vision volunteer to do things better,
giving him/her that specific responsibility, and
then quietly withdrawing the good will and
support which is offered to everyone else.

This works best with those who have a specific
idea for what needs to be done and who will
welcome a chance to prove themselves.

--Drumming them out by not re-electing, reap-
pointing, or reinviting. Making the
love-it-or-leave-it atmosphere so pervasive that
they will remove themselves from the situation.

This action is another way to insure the
unbridled proliferation of organizations and the
continuation of that bulwark of American culture: cutthroat competition.

--Drumming them in and letting groupthink take its
course. Inviting the operations volunteer to
have coffee with the staff or putting that board
member on the executive committee; making them
feel like one of the gang.

This works best with the more innocent who only
raised a question, who did not intend to start
World War III, and who will be relieved to learn

more about why we cannot do things any differently.

These are counterproductive not only because they
are demeaning to all parties involved but because they
preclude assessment of the merits in the issue/question
being raised. They are tremendously effective in the
short run in promoting a veneer of harmony.

Far more productive over the long haul are those
strategies which reflect a commitment to the crazy quilt
process and a desire to use all resources including the
vision volunteers which will build bridges from what is
to what could be. Some of these are:

--Evaluating the idea being offered. If it is an
answerable question, answering it. If it
requires further inquiry, pursuing it and
inviting the initiator to help. Making sure to
follow up and report back.

--If the idea generates new avenues for action,
pursuing them. If appropriate, reassigning the
vision volunteer to help implement the new
ideas. Recognizing that new ideas need as much
support and attention as old ones. Remembering
also that sometimes the people who generate new
ideas are not the best ones to implement them.

--If, after much mutual effort, the differences
prove "irreconcilable," encouraging the vision
volunteer to move on and into some other
setting--not with a sigh of victory or relief but
with sincere best wishes.

Obviously the lines between the counterproductive
and the productive are fine and hard to draw. Obviously
those who are vision volunteers are no less obligated to
act responsibly and accountably than other volunteers
and are not necessarily any more enlightened. However,
on the chance that they are onto something useful and in
the belief that different perceptions are essential,
vision volunteers are too important a resource to
ignore. To make better use of vision volunteering is
not to eliminate tension but to keep that tension
creative. It is not to rule out anger and frustration

but to keep them from becoming addictive and immobilizing.

It may seem excessively generous to call such nuisance activity "vision volunteering." In a very real sense all volunteers fall under this heading, since their involvement stems from perceptions of what is and what could be. This kind of "dreaming" is to be encouraged. Furthermore we should not exclude or excuse staff from opportunities and obligations to ask questions and seek new and better ways to function. Indeed many staff may well meet the same kinds of resistance and have even more to risk than volunteers if they get too far off the beaten path. The use of the term "vision volunteering" is primarily intended to counteract the very negative reception often given these "misfits" and to emphasize how important it is to refine our notions of what constitutes a "fit."

CAUTION: VISION VOLUNTEERING MAY BE HAZARDOUS TO HEALTH.

Even if we learn to make better use of vision volunteering for our larger purposes, being a vision volunteer, i.e., out of sync, is always expensive emotionally. One is trying to stay in the kitchen and stand the heat, thereby running the risk of getting burned. Effective use of vision volunteering will require organizations not only to be more accepting of change but also more assertive in making it happen. It is always easier to let someone else do it. At least you know whom to blame, if the changes do not produce miracles.

9.6 MOVING ON

Cynics could have a field day with all the ideas presented in this chapter, summing up the main points as follows:

--Promoting Volunteer Liberation: Peddling Meddling Licenses

--Appealing to Enlightened Self-Interest: Endorsing Me First

    --Developing Alternate Structures: Playing the Shell Game with "Appropriate Action" as the Elusive Pea.

    --Cultivating Vision Volunteers: Taking a Trojan Horse to Lunch.

    --VOLUNTEERING MAY BE HAZARDOUS TO HEALTH.

They may be right and can enjoy a good chuckle from their armchairs. The pessimistic or lazy will allow themselves to be thrown into fits of despondency and inactivity because they cannot see past all the problems.

Those who, having examined the same scene, choose to remain in the arena of action can learn to make more and better judgments while being less judgmental, can see many opportunities and challenges as well as problems and pitfalls, and can act with confidence rather than cockiness to make today's crazy quilt a little better than yesterday's even though it may not be as good as tomorrow's. The demands of building a free, democratic, pluralistic and responsive society compel us to move on. If all our experience to date suggests anything, it is that

NOT VOLUNTEERING MAY BE HAZARDOUS TO OUR HEALTH
AS INDIVIDUALS AND AS A SOCIETY.

RESOURCES

Dodson, Dan W. NEW CHALLENGES TO SOCIAL AGENCY LEADER-SHIP. South Plainfield, N.J.: Groupwork Today, Inc., 1976.

Gaylin, Willard; Glasser, Ira; Marcus, Steven; and Rothman, David. DOING GOOD: THE LIMITS OF BENE-VOLENCE. New York: Pantheon Books, 1978.

Goldston, Eli. THE QUANTIFICATION OF CONCERN: SOME ASPECTS OF SOCIAL ACCOUNTING. Pittsburgh: Carnegie Press, 1974.

Schindler-Rainman, Eva and Lippitt, Ronald. BUILDING THE COLLABORATIVE COMMUNITY: MOBILIZING CITIZENS FOR ACTION. Riverside, CA: University of California Extension, 1980.

Sheehy, Gail. PATHFINDERS: OVERCOMING THE CRISES OF ADULT LIFE AND FINDING YOUR OWN PATH TO WELL-BEING. New York: William Morrow and Company, Inc., 1981.

10

COMMON SENSE, COMMON DECENCY, AND THE
COMMON GOOD: A PERSONAL POSTSCRIPT

It is with a great sense of relief that I move back into the first person for a brief wrap-up of this exploration of various perspectives on volunteering. Writing a book about volunteering has been as exhausting and exhilarating as doing volunteer work or working with volunteers. Reading one may have had one or both of these effects also. There have been other parallels as illustrated by some experiences which occurred during the writing.

--Some days my sense of mission about why I must stick with it despite interruptions and obstacles was very clear. On some days it was so compelling that the resulting self-righteousness made it easy to come on strong about what must be done in the realm of volunteering and to risk the kick in the teeth that such arrogance may deserve. Other days I was not quite so sure and would gladly have settled for a pat on the head and a "Golly, she means well."

--I have brought to both writing and volunteer work my best thinking, my best value judgments, my best skills, my best experiences, and my most serious commitment. Yet my best has not been enough, if by "enough" I were to mean producing definitive solutions to all the problems under consideration. Chances of this book doing harm while I have tried to do good are probably minimal except to the possible extent of having wasted your time and mine. In other words, an awareness of "optimum" is burdensome as well as liberating.

--Speaking of self-serving (which is what I have just been), I have also spent considerable time in and around the volunteering I was doing while working on the book calculating who owed me the courtesy of buying my book solely on the grounds of all the hard work I had done with and for them. How many chips will I be able to call in to boost sales at least in my home community? So much for altruism.

--One's perspective is often influenced by strange, unrelated things. While I was working on Chapter 6, I developed back problems which made sitting and concentrating difficult. I drafted the section on standing committees literally standing at an ironing board which had proved to be the work surface of appropriate height to accommodate my condition. At one point I had this flash of insight: Perhaps if standing committee members actually stood for the duration of their meetings, they might learn to be a bit more efficient. At the time it seemed too facetious to include in a serious discussion of a genuinely serious problem. I include it now (a) to offer you some well-earned comic relief; (b) to remind us that, while volunteering is serious business, it does not have to be somber; (c) maybe it was not such a ridiculous notion; or (d) all of the above.

--It is hard to practice what you preach. Knowing that my "vision" is not in best focus on a certain worthy cause, I nonetheless succumbed to a friend's plea

206

to help organize a new group aimed at tackling a piece of that cause. I helped write bylaws, served as secretary, chaired the nominating committee, and did a few other chores. For reasons I do not fully understand, that is exactly how all the tasks felt--like chores. I never did develop the kind of passion which would sustain me or the organization if all it had was multiples of me. I "stuck out" my term and then made room for someone else. I know it was the right choice for me and am grateful that the future of the organization does not depend exclusively on me or on any one person.

Knowing that today's "professional volunteer" does not fall for the there's-not-much-to-it recruitment strategy, I promptly fell for it. The day I was to attend my first meeting as an advisory council member for another worthy cause, the chairman called in desperation and asked me to chair a standing committee. I asked what was involved; he said, "I'm not really sure. Not much though."; and on that basis I said yes. As it turns out, of course, there is quite a bit of work involved and this extra assignment puts me on the council's executive committee. This doubled the number of meetings I thought I would have to attend. For reasons which I do not fully understand, I am thoroughly enjoying the work which I was lulled into doing.

Whether I will actually be of any more value to Organization B because of greater enthusiasm than I was to Organization A remains to be seen and is not exclusively mine to measure. I do know it is easier to keep at the new assignment.

--By choosing to take a comprehensive look at volunteering as a complex social phenomenon, I have often felt that I had bitten off more than I could chew and had given myself a kind of intellectual indigestion for which only a handy ten-step guide on a particular facet would have spelled relief. This was compounded when friends and colleagues, bogged down with a particular volunteer-related problem, called for advice. They invariably prefaced their questions with "Are you dealing with . . . in your book?" Invariably my first response was, "Well, yes and no." Once I got over being embarrassed that I did not have instant expert advice, we settled into exchanges of questions, information, and perspectives which were beneficial to both of us. These conversations reinforced my conviction that we often know more about the "how-to" than about the "how-come" and "why bother." Mutual respect and support as well as know-how help keep us all going.

   --The risks and costs of writing as well as of volunteer work have been far outweighed by the increased self-awareness, personal growth and renewed energy generated by such exercise. I have learned that, while I believe all the aspects of volunteering I have explored are valid, the one I find personally most compelling and urgent is policy volunteering. Though I have, I hope, scrupulously avoided getting too involved in subject areas other than volunteering, I have learned more about which substantive issues I personally wish to pursue. In other words, I have recovered from my latest volunteer burnout and have put myself back on the hook of keeping volunteer work as an integral part of my life.

   This sojourn through the various perspectives and complex issues surrounding volunteerism may have proven at points to be overwhelming and/or depressing. I sincerely hope there have been just as many moments which produced new lines of thought and grounds for optimism. In case it has gotten lost along the way, it is important to conclude that meaning well is not enough, but meaning well is important. It is not a sufficient condition for improving society, but it is a necessary one.

   The common sense which tells even the most naive that there is still something out of kilter in society and which propels them into volunteer work has more going for it than we may have credited to it. Common decency and the common good are valuable concepts even if they cannot be precisely and universally defined. The much touted American voluntary spirit is alive but cannot be ignored or taken for granted. It deserves neither unqualified praise nor absolute condemnation. Volunteerism warrants the very best critiquing and commitment we can bring to it in pursuing the unfinished business of assuring human welfare, human dignity and social justice.

Effective volunteers will need to use all the sophistication and sensitivity they can muster. They can be assured that they will make mistakes, will be criticized, and will wonder if they are taking two steps backward for every one forward. In such moments they should reflect on one more piece of our legacy from Lady Bountiful: If she could have anticipated the coals over which her modest efforts would be raked, she would have been crazy not to stay home. She did the best she could with what she knew how to do. It clearly was not good enough. Yet it is equally clear that we were able to learn from her mistakes because she was willing to risk involvement. Would society have been more equitable and just if she had minded her own business?

APPENDIX A
DEFINING VOLUNTEER

As noted in Chapter 1, everybody knows what "volunteer" means until asked to define it. Then it takes about two sentences to become embroiled in semantic nitpicking which may seem as pointless as it is frustrating. This is particularly true for those who are not researchers exploring volunteerism as a socio-logical phenomenon but rather who are involved as or with volunteers in specific settings at specific times. In these cases it seems sufficient for all practical purposes to define "volunteer" as anyone we can get to pitch in on certain tasks without being paid in cash for his/her time and skills.

Yet this narrow perspective can lead to problems. For example, if this is our working definition and if unpaid slots in a given organization remain unfilled despite repeated pleas for help, it is easier to conclude that "people just are not volunteering anymore" than to look at those empty slots against a broader picture of volunteering. In that wider perspective we would have to confront the fact that a "no" to a specific recruitment pitch is not necessarily a rejection of volunteering. The problem may be in the nature of the slots. They may be noncompetitive for valid and correctable reasons. (See Chapters 5 through 8.) Thus for some practical purposes, a broader perspective and more encompassing definition may be necessary even if all we want to do is find enough help to get from today to tomorrow.

An adequate and comprehensive definition of volunteer is elusive, and a flawless one may be unattainable. Most raise as many quesions as they answer, as the following examples will illustrate.

1. Webster's New Collegiate Dictionary offers this:

> A volunteer is one who enters into or offers himself for a service of his own free will, as one who enters military service voluntarily or one who renders a service . . . while having no legal concern or interest.

While volunteer army is no doubt a clear concept since it is the one career choice which can be imposed on individuals by the government, this definition does not help distinguish between the volunteer soldier and the volunteer fireman. Nor does it differentiate between the employee who works two hours of overtime without pay and the employee who leaves work on time to serve for two hours as a Scout leader. Yet we would probably agree that such distinctions are necessary to understanding volunteerism.

2. In 1974, ACTION, the federal agency promoting citizen involvement, commissioned the Census Bureau to conduct a survey of volunteering. For purposes of this study, volunteering was defined as:

Unpaid work for an organization with
religious, political, social welfare,
health, education, civic and community
action, recreation, and justice purposes.[1]

Choice is implicit in this definition. While it comes
close to the common sense understanding of what
volunteer means, this definition does not take into
account volunteering done in a nonorganizational setting.

"Unpaid" is not such a straightforward concept
either. At what point does reimbursement of expenses
for services rendered become "pay"? Is a stipend
"pay"? Does it change the volunteer's status or
functioning? Are employees who are permitted two hours
a week of company time to work with the handicapped
"unpaid"? Should they be considered volunteers?

3. The Gallup Organization conducted a survey for
INDEPENDENT SECTOR in 1981 in which volunteer work was
broadly defined as:

Working in some way to help others for no
monetary pay.[2]

This definition was designed to include helping activities carried out informally or alone as well as those
undertaken for an organization. This broader definition
produced some interesting responses which might not fall
in everyone's concept of volunteering:

I baked brownies for my son's Cub Scout
troop.
I am an attorney, and I sometimes give
free advice to my neighbors.
I visit my sister who is in a mental
institution.[3]

The definition and the resulting survey did not
include membership in a volunteer group if no actual
work was done. Nor did it include participation in
co-operatives (such as nursery schools) where there is
monetary compensation because of the lower costs, though
not direct pay.

Like the ACTION survey, this one encompassed work done in various service areas: health, education, justice, citizenship, recreation, social welfare, community action, religious, political, arts and culture, work-related (unions and professional associations), informal-alone, and general fundraisers.

4. For their historical review of American volunteering, Ellis and Noyes defined the verb:

> To volunteer is to choose to act in recognition of a need with an attitude of social responsibility and without concern for monetary profit, going beyond what is necessary to one's immediate physical well-being.[4]

This definition shares with the previous ones the concepts of choice, social responsibility and absence of the profit motive. These writers stressed that social responsibility can only be defined by the volunteer and that the definition then can properly include vigilante and extremist groups whose methods may be questionable legally. Like the INDEPENDENT SECTOR definition, this one encompasses neighboring and informal activity, and it excludes membership and voting as being normally expected of all members/citizens. In other words, Ellis and Noyes view volunteer work as going beyond what is normally expected.

They have refined the "unpaid" concept somewhat so that it does incorporate Peace Corps "volunteers" or employees doing "volunteer" work on released time. But why is a Peace Corps volunteer any more of a "volunteer" than someone who chooses to make a career of a low-paying service profession? Is it more because it may be outside normal career paths than because of the subsistence pay? Ellis and Noyes included volunteer work which may have a positive impact on one's career but emphasized that any such rewards are not meant to equal the value of the service performed in the monetary sense.[5]

5. The definition being used in this book was designed to facilitate reflection as well as analysis.

A volunteer is an individual who chooses to participate in activities perceived by that person to promote human welfare, human dignity, and social justice when those activities
--are not the source of one's livelihood
--require involvement beyond what is expected of all citizens (e.g., voting) or of all members of an organization (e.g., paying dues),
--and are conducted in a manner consistent with the ideals of a free, democratic, pluralistic society.

While it contains many of the same themes as other definitions, it contains many value judgments made by a writer concerned with "effective" volunteering. For example the distinction between "without regard for monetary profit" and "not the source of one's livelihood" is an attempt to get around several issues:

a) Some people's jobs in human services are so underpaid that these persons might well be considered to be doing them without regard for monetary profit.

b) At least one means of earning a livelihood--being a housewife--is not directly related to monetary gain but is not volunteer work either.

c) A service activity may be undertaken with career advancement in mind but is still volunteer work if it is not the source of take-home pay AND it involves a social need.

The last clause about volunteer work encompassing only those activities which are consistent with the ideals of a free society was included to remind writer and reader:

a) that not all voluntary activity is volunteer work,

b) that not all volunteer work and voluntary activity is healthy and constructive for society simply because the volunteer did not have to do it and/or did it without pay,

c) and that, while individual volunteers act on their own perceptions of need, we all need to make judgments about whether or not the impact of "meaning well" actually contributes to the common good.

The important thing to remember about any definition is not its inherent perfection but its usefulness for the purposes intended. The dictionary reflects common usage. The ACTION and INDEPENDENT SECTOR definitions were devised for counting purposes. Ellis and Noyes were doing a historical review of voluntary activity as a social force in American society, for better or worse. This writer is analyzing the phenomenon with an eye to evaluating myths and realities in volunteering and to pointing us toward better performance. Rather than seeking perfection, it may be more productive to exercise greater precision in interpreting any data and insights which each definition generates.

REFERENCES

[1]U.S. Census Bureau, AMERICANS VOLUNTEER 1974: A STATISTICAL STUDY OF VOLUNTEERS IN THE UNITED STATES (Washington, D.C.: ACTION, February, 1975), p. 9.

[2]The Gallup Organization, Inc., AMERICANS VOLUNTEER 1981: A STUDY CONDUCTED FOR INDEPENDENT SECTOR, (Princeton, N.J.: The Gallup Organization, June, 1981), p. i.

[3]IBID., p. iii.

[4]Susan J. Ellis and Katherine H. Noyes, BY THE PEOPLE: A HISTORY OF AMERICANS AS VOLUNTEERS (Philadelphia: ENERGIZE, 1978), p. 10.

[5]IBID.

APPENDIX B
MEASURING VOLUNTEERING

Measuring the scope of volunteering is no simpler than defining volunteer in the abstract. Naturally any measurement is based on a definition and is therefore limited by and to it. Like different definitions, different measurements do have uses and strengths. Let us look at some of the questions and answers which some measurements give us and thereby add methodological nitpicking to the semantic variety of Appendix A.

1. Counting

Two of the definitions we examined earlier were used as a basis for counting the number of Americans who volunteer and the percentage of the population which

216

this number represents. As already indicated, a study such as the 1974 ACTION survey which encompasses only organized volunteering automatically excludes volunteering which is done informally or alone. As a result, it underestimates the scope of voluntary service activity.

The 1981 INDEPENDENT SECTOR study attempted to address this by including questions which ascertained whether the volunteer work was done on an organized or unorganized basis and by evaluating findings for each category. However, since what constitutes informal volunteering is open to such a wide range of subjective definitions, the accuracy of the measurement can be questioned. For example, one person may call baking cookies for a child's Scout troop volunteering. Yet another who has also baked cookies for the same purpose may perceive it as parenting and not report it in a volunteer survey. Did this survey then also underestimate the scope of volunteering? If so, does it matter?

Aside from definitions, other factors have to be understood in order to determine the usefulness of any head count of volunteers. A major one is when and for what period the questions are asked. Surveys generally ask respondents if they did volunteer work during a specific time period. If that period was recent (e.g., last week or during the last three months), answers might be more reliable because people might have better recall. However, the specified time period might be atypical. For example, the 1974 survey asked about volunteer work done during a week in which both Easter and Passover fell. This led to questions as to whether or not religious volunteering was out of proportion to normal. Also some types of volunteering are seasonal. Education volunteering is concentrated during the school year whereas certain recreation volunteering takes place primarily in the summer. Political activity waxes and wanes depending on election dates.

On the other hand, if you ask people to enumerate all the volunteer work they have done in the last twelve months or to compare what they do now with what they did three years ago (as INDEPENDENT SECTOR did), they may not remember everything accurately paticularly if their volunteer work generally falls in the cookie baking category.

217

Some statistics, if viewed as a count of volunteers, may overestimate the number of people involved. For example, the American Association of Fund Raising Counsel issues reports on the number of volunteers who worked in twenty leading national charities such as Scouts and Y's. There are two problems with construing any such figures as measures of volunteering or as trends in volunteering.

a) There may be duplication. In 1979, this writer would have been counted four times. It was a busy year.

b) This approach measures not just organized volunteering but organized volunteering in traditional, "establishment" groups. (Chapter 4 discusses the growth of anti-establishment volunteering.)

It must be noted that AAFRC makes no claim that these figures "count" volunteering. Any misuse of this or other data to conclude that people really do or do not volunteer anymore is on the part of the data consumers.

2. Other Survey Information

Major surveys collect information on aspects of volunteering other than "Did you or didn't you?".

a) Type of work done. This usually means what issue/subject area the volunteer works in such as religion, social welfare, education. None of the surveys have done much on distinguishing among the nature of tasks done: direct service, board and committee work.

b) How much volunteering is done, usually expressed in hours per week.

c) Demographic variables which may influence the choice of volunteer work and the amount of time spent: Age, socio-economic status, marital status, education level, type of community.

d) Reasons why people do or do not start volunteering and reasons why they do or do not continue to volunteer.

The wealth of such data contained in the ACTION and INDEPENDENT SECTOR surveys cannot be adequately summarized here. At first glance they seem to reinforce what "everybody" already knows about volunteers. For example, the "typical" volunteer is female, middle- or upper-class, well-educated, middle-aged. People get involved because they want to do something useful, enjoy the work they do, or have a child involved. They quit because the project ended, they became too busy, or the child moved on to other things.

But under closer scrutiny there are many other implications for assessing the societal impact of volunteering and for determining what types of people are attracted to what kinds of volunteer work and why. Everyone associated with volunteering would benefit from a close look at these surveys and their results.

It must be kept in mind that the surveys show correlations not causal relationships and that they cannot accurately be compared with one another to show trends because the definitions and questions varied just enough to leave us with the old apples-and-oranges problem.

3. Dollar Value of Volunteer Work

Attempts have been made to express in dollars the contribution of volunteer work to the nation's economy. Such measures start with definitions and data whose limits we have already discussed. To these it is necessary to add still more assumptions about the value of the work.

Perhaps the simplest dollar translation is to multiply hours reported by the minimum wage. This is what INDEPENDENT SECTOR did to estimate the value of teen volunteer time.[1] Using minimum wage as a base for this age group may be appropriate since employed teens would be likely to be paid at this level. However, as a general measure, it could be criticized for not differentiating among different types of volunteer work and the relative amount of skill each entails. The minimum wage approach probably leads to an underestimation of the economic value of volunteer time.

For adult volunteers INDEPENDENT SECTOR looked at that volunteer work done in a structured setting and at the education level of the volunteers. For each educational grouping they multiplied the hours worked by the then prevailing average hourly wage for all workers with the same level of education.[2]

Here again the figure bears no relation to what the actual work done by the volunteers might have cost if society had had to "bid" for it in the marketplace. By this measure, a corporate executive who washed dishes at a benefit spaghetti supper would have made a greater dollar contribution than a high school dropout doing the same thing. One may assume and may be correct that the executive would not have done this work at all if pay were the issue and that his/her time is considered more valuable. Nevertheless, the measurement approach raises questions about overestimating the value of volunteer services.

In an earlier effort, Harold Wolozin was asked to extrapolate from the 1974 ACTION survey data an estimate of the dollar value of volunteer work reported therein. He pointed out that any wage figure underestimates cost because it does not include fringe benefit expenses. He chose instead to use an hourly compensation figure which he and his cohorts believed represented the closest occupational match to the volunteer work being performed. For his purposes, that meant the average of the mean hourly compensation for employees in:

> wholesale and retail trade
> finance, insurance, and real estate
> services

His report acknowledges the severe lack of data about the exact nature of the work being performed and the need for such information.[3]

In general, dollar values are hampered by the lack of this kind of data. Even if we knew precisely what work volunteers do, however, translations into dollar figures are not automatic. What would you use to estimate the worth of time spent in board and committee

220

work? Board members of for-profit corporations are compensated. Is there something in how they are paid which could be applied to the nonprofit sector?

Use of dollar data for trend analysis is further complicated by the challenge of using comparable bases for dollar value.

4. So What?

Despite their methodological limitations, all of these efforts are to be commended for the pioneering they have done rather than condemned for what they have not done. They have several important uses.

First, they provide valuable information for those "in the field" which may help in assessing who volunteers, why they volunteer, and what areas of community service they are attracted to. This information can facilitate discussion of and insight into the implication for a particular area. For example, why do both the 1974 and 1981 studies show "justice" at the bottom of the list? Are justice-related concerns not perceived as urgent? Is there no demand for volunteers to work in these fields? Do the volunteer jobs and/or the clients intimidate people?

Secondly, the figures are startling and can be used with honesty for various public relations purposes. Though we have poked at the inadequacies of measurement, the figures do show that volunteering is a significant force at work in society. They dramatically make the point that volunteering should not be taken for granted or ignored. If it builds morale to tell a small group of volunteers that they are part of a marvelous minority which has collectively contributed 7.8 billion hours[4] of service nationwide, then do it. If you can support your case for better funding of volunteer programs by pointing out that your costs are a veritable drop in the bucket compared to the $64.5 billion[5] that in 1980-1981 we did not have to pay in taxes or charitable contributions because volunteers did the work, then do it. Just refrain from overdoing it and from making comparisons among various sets of figures.

Finally, if we get to a point where we have better measurement tools or if the same study were conducted more than once, we would get some very useful comparative data. Who knows? We might find out for sure if more (or fewer) people are volunteering. If we see changes in the subject areas where volunteers work, we may have a better idea about what items are high on the volunteers' social agendas and what shifts in priority have occurred, if any.

Better measurement of volunteering is one important factor of a larger attempt to clarify the role and impact of the entire voluntary sector. It is quite possible that our traditional indicators have been inadequate because they have overlooked the impact of volunteering as an economic institution. It is important to all of us that some of us keep at the challenge of defining and measuring.

REFERENCES

[1] INDEPENDENT SECTOR, News Release, (Washington, D.C., January 7, 1982), p. 2.

[2] IBID.

[3] Harold Wolozin, THE VALUE OF VOLUNTEER SERVICES IN THE UNITED STATES, (Washington, D.C.: ACTION, September 1976), ACTION Pamphlet No. 35304, pp. 15-16.

[4] INDEPENDENT SECTOR News Release, OP. CIT.

[5] IBID.

INDEX